"BESETTING SIN" OF CHURCH

Forceful Address at Shrewsbury Service

Many people were unable to gain admission to St. John's Hill Method. Church, Shrewsbury, which was crowded, on Tuesday, for the visit of the Rev. Dr. Martyn Lloyd-Jones, of Westminster Chapel, who preached at evening and afternoon services, arranged by the Shropshire Free Church Federal Council. An appeal launched by the council for funds to cover a deficiency and to raise a credit balance had already brought in £72, and the collections from Tuesday's service realised a further £58.

At the afternoon service, Dr. Lloyd-Jones, said that what he regarded as "besetting sin of the Church today"

Stornoway Gazette Sep 5. 1964

OUTSTANDING PREACHER

Rev. Martin Lloyd-Jones For Stornoway

One of the most outstanding preachers in Great Britain today, Rev. D. Martin Lloyd-Jones will be preaching in Stornoway on Monday and Tuesday of next week. The Free Church will be used as the main venue for the meetings and in addition Martin's Memorial Church and the Free Church Seminary will be linked by loudspeaker unit to enable [...] to take part in the [...]

It may also be the [...] Dr. Lloyd-Jones [...] at the two overflow meetings in the [...] either before or at a meeting in the [...]

appeal is made to [...] be fortunate enough [...] in the Free Church [...] and who wish to [...] following evening [...] seats in the overflow [...] that those who [...] unable to get seats [...] on the Monday evening [...] do so.

[...]tion will be taken [...] the three places to [...]nses and [...] he Scotti[...]

Time [...] entering [...]-Jones [...] practised [...]arley Str[...] with [...] to the [...] from the [...]wever, a [...] when [...] feel that [...]ouls had [...]han the s[...]rned to [...]Theologi[...]

A Great Religious Gathering

CW00460141

[...] the [...] communion season [...] of coaches and scores of [...] brought in the people from all over the North of Scotland, including Skye and the Hebrides. The spacious Church was full to overflowing on the Sabbath evening, when extra chairs and forms had to be brought in.

The centre of attraction was the Rev. Dr D. Martyn Lloyd-Jones from London. He was the man of whom the Moderator of the Presbytery said: "In the field of medicine he had the ball at his feet, but gave it all up when he felt the call to preach the Gospel." Those who were privileged to listen, heard what was probably the greatest preaching heard in these parts this century. One of the most striking features of Dr Lloyd-Jones' presentation of the Gospel was the way he showed how relevant the Gospel is to the present day and how hollow and illogical is "Modern Man" who rejects it.

In a 72-minute sermon of extraordinary power, delivered on the Tuesday evening, on the "Rich Fool," the modern man who rejected Christianity was seen in his true colours. He was a fool because in his thinking he left out the two most important issues in life, death, and God. The fact was [...] n with all [...]ries and to [...]le no prov[...]

Dr. Lloyd-Jones at Corsham

There was a large congregation on Monday evening at the Corsham Congregational Church, when a special visit was paid by Dr. Martyn Lloyd-Jones, of Westminster Chapel, London. Every available space in the building and gallery was occupied. The Rev. S. I. Lippiatt took the first part of the service, and gave a welcome to Dr. Lloyd-Jones. The choir rendered [...]

HIS "FIERY" SPEECH

Dr. Lloyd Jones was preaching in Brunswick Chapel at the final day of the annual convention of Newcastle and District Free Church Council in Newcastle yesterday when a box of matches in a pocket of his waistcoat burst into flames.

With the help of the Rev. H. T. Donaldson he extinguished the "outbreak" in a few moments, and although the garment was damaged he continued his address.

Bi[...] Ra[...] Cro[...]

IN all my religious [...] Glasgow [...] nothing more [...] than the Bible [...] held this week [...]

On Tuesday [...] longest queues [...] not at cinemas [...] entertainment, b[...] Andrew's Hall, [...] eager to secure a [...] great Rally. Af[...] been packed in [...] was estimated [...] people had to [...] Nor was it wholl[...] a crowd of "gr[...] The proportion o[...] impressed every [...]

What was the [...] attracted such [...] aim was define[...] proclaim belief t[...] the Word of Go[...] the nation to th[...] ing and study of [...] only one of the k[...] of the kind ever [...] but it was one of [...] Never, perhaps [...] assembled under [...] time so many r[...] so many differe[...] atmosphere was [...] but evangelical.

JANUARY 19, 19[...]

THEOLOGICAL ST[...] CONFERENCE (I.[...] CAMBRIDG[...]

(From a Correspo[...])

THE leaders of the I.V.F[...] of the Conference he[...] from January 1-4 affir[...] best for years past. The [...] the spiritual were refres[...] The Conference owed more [...] to the deep spirituality and [...] with which the host, Dr. L[...] Jones, guided the discussi[...] brilliance of his searching [...] Place of Preaching in the C[...] and "Preaching the [...] To-day." The latter par[...] massive and prophetic conc[...] The intellectual side of th[...]

[Left margin fragments:]
[...]ked Wivern School [...]rn School to hear Dr. [...] considered [...]chers and me. Cars [...] afield as [...]-Somerset. [...]wlish, and [...] he school, the build[...], balcony, [...]g into ad[...]ed by a [...]er of the [...]fellowship, [...]hich comp[...], Bible [...]s a great [...]loyd-Jones one-time

D. MARTYN LLOYD-JONES

Letters 1919–1981

Selected with Notes
by
Iain H. Murray

THE BANNER OF TRUTH TRUST

THE BANNER OF TRUTH TRUST ·
3 Murrayfield Road, Edinburgh EH12 6EL
PO Box 621, Carlisle, Pennsylvania 17013, USA

*

© Lady Catherwood & Ann Desmond 1994
First Published 1994
ISBN 0 85151 674 2

*

Typeset in 11/13 pt Bembo
Printed and bound in Great Britain
at The Bath Press, Avon

CONTENTS

2: To His Wife

3: To Friends and Fellow Ministers

4: *Westminster Chapel*

5: *Some Family Letters*

6: *A Younger Generation and New Agencies*

7: On Evangelical Unity and the Threat of Ecumenism

8: Queries and Controversies

9: The 'Retirement' Years

BIOGRAPHICAL TABLE

1899   Born in Cardiff, South Wales, 20 December.

1906–14   Childhood in Llangeitho, Cardiganshire.

1914–16   London and Marylebone Grammar School.

1916–21   Medical student at St Bartholomew's Hospital.

1921   Becomes Assistant to the Royal Physician, Sir
            Thomas Horder.

1925–26   Struggles over the call to preach.

1927   Marriage to Bethan Phillips.
            Minister of Sandfields, Aberavon, Port Talbot.

1937   Second visit to North America.

1938   Resigns from Sandfields. Later becomes temporary
            assistant to Dr G. Campbell Morgan, Westminster
            Chapel, London.

1939   Second World War begins the day before ML-J
            was to be formally inducted as co-pastor of
            Westminster Chapel.
            President of Inter-Varsity Fellowship of Students.

1940–41   Westminster Chapel struggling to survive the effects
            of evacuation and bombing.

1943   Retirement of Dr Campbell Morgan from West-
            minster Chapel. Removal from Haslemere to
            Colebrooke Avenue, Ealing.

1945   Formal opening of the Evangelical Library in
            London. Removal to Mount Park Crescent,
            Ealing.

1947	Third visit to North America. Chairman of the International Fellowship of Evangelical Students.
1950	Starts Sermon on the Mount series. First Puritan Conference at Westminster Chapel.
1953	Attacked in the *British Weekly* on the publication of his IVF address, 'Maintaining the Evangelical Faith Today'.
1959	*Studies in the Sermon on the Mount*, first major volume of expository sermons.
1965	Removal to Creffield Road, Ealing.
1966	'Evangelical Unity': Call for an evangelical response to ecumenism.
1967	Keele Congress: Anglican evangelicals announce a new policy. Westminster Chapel joins the British Evangelical Council and the FIEC.
1968	Illness suddenly closes his ministry at Westminster Chapel with his 372nd and last exposition of Romans.
1969	Last visit to the United States. Addresses on 'Preaching' (later published in *Preachers and Preaching*).
1970	First volume of his *Romans* series published.
1971	Last visit to Continent and addresses for IFES, 'What is an Evangelical?'. Westminster Conference replaces the Puritan Conference.
1980	Preaches in June for last time.
1981	Dies at Ealing on 1 March.

INTRODUCTION

Dr Lloyd-Jones is best known in the world today for his books and yet the last role in which he ever envisaged himself was that of an author. When an address by him was being published in 1939 he regarded it with some humour. He genuinely thought of himself as 'a mere speaker'. He never used a typewriter and wrote very little. None of his published works began life with that end in view. They were delivered as sermons or addresses and would never have appeared in print at all if it had not been for the short-hand transcriptions or tapes which survived to make it possible. A comparison of the date when such material was first spoken with the date when it was first printed, often ten or twenty years later, makes that very clear. At least one reason why he never responded to a call for an autobiography was that sitting down to write would have been alien to the habits of a lifetime. It is well-known that his dedication was to the pulpit, but in addition to that he was always enthusiastic for the medium of the spoken word, whether in face to face conversations or in telephone calls. Both played a major part in his life. In contrast the pen was his last resort.

The knowledge of that fact partially explains why some of us overlooked until now the possibility of a volume of his correspondence. The very existence of sufficient letters suitable for publication seemed doubtful. He never had a full-time secretary and did not make a practice of keeping copies of the letters which he wrote. It was therefore of some surprise to us to realise that, with the possible exception of sermon notes, he wrote letters more than he wrote anything else. In words from his own hand, these letters confirm that his assessment of himself was as I have suggested above. We find him writing to E. T. Rees in 1926, 'I am a poor correspondent at the best of times', and to Philip Hughes in South

Africa in 1945, 'I warned you before you left that I am a truly bad correspondent'. The many who received letters from him simply stating his time of arrival for services away from London, or covering such-like things, might agree with that opinion. These communications were short and to the point. But the surprise to us has been the number of letters which do not fall into that category and, when we began to gather these together, it became apparent that a volume of his personal correspondence would be of interest and value to many.

The fact is that there were many factors which constantly over-rode his reluctance to take up a pen. The first was his intense affection for his wife and family. If he was away from Bethan for more than a day or two he always wrote and generally at some length. She was in every sense a partner in all that he did. Although a medical doctor herself, she happily gave her life to keeping him preaching and to the care of the home. His mother also had many letters from him. He always kept in touch with her when she was away from her London home, generally in her beloved Cardiganshire. At such times he usually wrote to her weekly. From their early years his daughters, Elizabeth and Ann, had notes from him when he was away and when they became students at Oxford they had a letter practically every week. This continued for Elizabeth when she married in 1954 and moved to the North of England. Forty years later she still recalls how Tuesday morning was looked forward to as the day his letter came. I hope enough of these letters have been included in this book to reveal how much all these family relationships meant to him. Any neglect of family on the part of ministers or missionaries he regarded as a very serious failure in biblical Christianity.

A pastor's heart was another constant factor which made correspondence a necessity for him. As the following pages show, sympathy and concern for people, whoever they might be, comes out in so many of his letters. He was for ever giving counsel and advice, and I believe never failed to respond to any appeal of that kind. Nor was this counsel in anyway stereotyped. When he knew the individual concerned, the opinion he gave was always wisely related to his insight into their character. He was always so generous in praise of points where he perceived strength that he constantly gave people the confidence that their problems or troubles could be overcome.

An illustration of the extent to which he would go to help men can be seen in his letter of 23 September 1964 to the Rev. J. Gwyn-Thomas in which he puts before him the prospect of his moving to another Church of England living. That instance is also a reminder of how he did not make his own conscience a rule for others. He was no advocate of patronage as a way to settle ministers, nor of an Established Church, but if another evangelical minister was able to accept such things he was ready to try to help him find a better sphere of usefulness.

I have drawn repeatedly in this collection from the close-on seventy surviving letters which Dr Lloyd-Jones wrote to Philip Hughes. While there is no parallel collection from his pen to anyone else, these letters, and others in the present volume, are typical of so many which were motivated by an eagerness to help colleagues and to encourage younger men. All over Britain and beyond, there were men in the ministry whose work and steadfastness owed more than they could say to the friendship which he extended to them. The greater part of his ministry in this regard was done by personal meetings and phone calls, but a number of the letters here reprinted provide a permanent indication of why his counsel meant so much to so many.

The majority of the letters now published were written by hand. Only in 1946 did he begin to use a very part-time secretary. Gradually from that date he began to dictate letters; never to family and only sometimes to close friends. It has to be admitted that in terms of *readability* there was a universe of difference between the letters he wrote and those which he dictated! Nonetheless his own hand was greatly prized by his correspondents not least because a high sense of achievement belonged to the few who had mastered, or thought they had mastered, his handwriting! The story goes that a minister's wife in Wales at first took a near-indecipherable note arriving in the post to be a notification from the Chinese laundry. Closer examination revealed that it was from Dr Lloyd-Jones, giving his time of arrival for anniversary services. Mrs Lloyd-Jones' advice to any bemused correspondent who had to face her husband's hand was not to attempt to read single words; one had to 'take a run at a line', and when really stumped have a break before returning to the problem with an open mind.

As the reader will soon see, in correspondence, as in some other matters, ML-J did not give up some of the norms which existed in his Edwardian youth. More particularly, he never regarded 'formalities' as inimical to true friendship. Outside the family it was very rare indeed for him to sign a letter with his Christian name, 'Martyn'. Similarly, he addressed his friend Douglas Johnson for years as 'My Dear Dr Johnson', softening it somewhat later to 'My Dear Sir'. 'My Dear Sir', as Douglas Johnson knew, was a term of affection from ML-J. His many letters to Leslie Land began 'Dear Mr Land', but soon moved to 'My Dear Land' and that was the title which remained. Some five years of correspondence had passed between Land and ML-J before the latter added a P.S. to a letter saying, 'Please address me as just "Lloyd-Jones" in future'. Philip Hughes had the unique experience of passing from 'Dear Mr Hughes', through 'My dear Friend', to 'My dear Philip', all within one year!

For nearly all the letters here printed I am indebted to the correspondents who received them and made them available to me. Especial gratitude belongs to the late Bethan Lloyd-Jones for not only making personal letters available but also for translating the passages which he wrote to her in Welsh. I must also thank Dr Lloyd-Jones' daughters, Lady Catherwood and Mrs Ann Desmond both for the use of letters and for all their help in many other ways. Without the access they have given me to family archives I would have been greatly limited both in this and in the previous volumes of biography. It is anticipated that these archives and the originals of his correspondence will ultimately be housed in the National Library of Wales at Aberystwyth. May I ask any who have letters of any substance which we have not seen if they would kindly send them, or copies of them, to me at the address of the present publishers. I will see that in due course they are housed with other Lloyd-Jones papers.

I must make clear that this is only a representative selection from surviving correspondence. I have deliberately not used all his letters which were published earlier in his biography, though this volume would have been the poorer if some of the most important had not been included again here. In making the selection I have tried to show the breadth of his interests. There is a considerable contrast, for example, in the contents of his letters to his country-loving mother, with their talk of people, crops, farms and horses, and those to correspondents who wanted to know such things as his opinion on Barth or Niebuhr! I have also been impressed afresh at how much of his character as a Christian comes through in so many incidental ways in these letters. It is in part for that reason that these letters are unedited. While some sentences might have been removed without any loss I have preferred to leave that judgment to the reader. Letters, unlike biographies, are likely to include the ordinary but in some respects that is to our advantage for as Pascal says, 'Man's virtue must not be judged by great occasions, but by his ordinary life'.

In Dr Lloyd-Jones' published sermons and addresses we see a Luther-like readiness to stand firm, and if need be alone, for the truth. But here, in a thousand ways, are indications of the attractiveness of his everyday humanity, and especially of his kindness and consideration for others. The latter characteristic goes far to explain why so often he retained the friendship and esteem even of those with whom he differed. The reader will find for instance in these pages a rather critical letter written to the late Professor Donald MacKay. It was Professor MacKay himself who provided us with this letter, sending with it his own testimony of what the ministry of ML-J had meant to him.

There are also sidelights of information in these letters of considerable historical significance. Nothing has struck me more about the difference between the writer's day and our own than the references to his mid-week services in many parts of Britain. Such mid-week services, attended by many hundreds, and sometimes thousands, have all but disappeared today. Social reasons may partly account for the change, but fundamentally the difference has to be connected with a decline in interest in the preaching of the Word of God. An era has passed away. But these letters will be a reminder that when God raises up a man whose heart is full of love, and whose lips have been touched with heavenly fire, there will always be a readiness to hear.

It remains for me to thank the Rev. Elwyn Davies for providing translation from the Welsh where it was necessary in the letters he received from Dr Lloyd-Jones, and Mr Dafydd Ifans for drawing our attention to Welsh sources which we would have missed. These included the two important letters to the Editor of *Barn* which Mr Ifans has translated for us.

Iain H. Murray
Edinburgh, September 1994

1

THE EARLY YEARS

Hospital and Family News

St Bartholomew's Hospital,
London E.C.1
Friday, 18 July, 1919

[To his Mother][1]
My dear Mamma,

Again I am writing without having much news to give you. I would have written earlier in the week but for the fact that I have been extremely busy. As I think I pointed out before, I was on duty over the weekend so that I was kept very busy until Wednesday. Since then also, I have been very busy with operations to attend etc. Added to these I caught another nasty cold last weekend, so that I have been feeling very tired. However, it is much better by now; with the rest over this week-end, I hope to be all right once more.

I am very glad to hear that you are enjoying yourself so much, and I suppose that you have been to Llangeitho by now.

I do not know exactly how I am going to spend to-morrow. I feel that in view of my cold it would perhaps be advisable for me not to play tennis as it might get worse. At the same time I do not feel like standing in the crowd watching the procession. Of course, the peace celebrations will not make much difference to you down there.

Well, Harcombe has now left London for good. He was discharged Wednesday morning and went home yesterday. It was

---

[1] The earliest letter which has survived. His mother (Magdalene) was on holiday near Newcastle Emlyn.

very amusing to watch him listening to D. O. Evans speaking on Tuesday night in our house. Of course after D. O. went, he broke out. The same night Tom Hugh Jones called round. Mary Jane has undergone the operation and is going on all right, but on opening her up they found out that it was not an 'ovarian cyst' at all, but tuberculosis of the peritoneum, which means tuberculosis of the membranous lining of all the viscera. It is a very serious condition although not as serious as tuberculosis of the lung. She will probably have to go to a sanatorium and have the ordinary treatment. It is hard to tell which way it will turn out. She may recover completely, but on the other hand she may die very suddenly. They are worrying terribly about it, and their Doctor has given them to understand that it was absolutely hopeless. However, I have had several cases of it and some of them have done quite well, and got quite all right, and on reading up I find that the text-books say the same thing.

Well, I must stop now if I want to catch this post. I will write to you over the weekend.

With fondest love to you and all down there. I remain,

Your loving son,

Martyn

Controversy over 'The Tragedy of Modern Wales'

7 Regency Street,
Westminster, London S.W.
10 February, 1925

[To Mr Ieuan Phillips][1]
My dear Ieuan,

You are probably well aware of the fact that I really have a good excuse this time for not answering your exceptionally nice letter long before this. I assume you have seen the *South Wales News* the

---

[1] Ieuan Phillips, his future brother-in-law, to whom he early became attached at the Calvinistic Chapel in Charing Cross Road, London, to which they both belonged. At this date Ieuan was studying for the ministry of the Calvinistic Methodist Church at Aberystwyth.

last few days and can therefore understand that what with people calling and phoning I have had very little time to myself.[1]

Last week, of course, I was well occupied with my paper and I want to tell you some of the facts.

I have already made up my mind as to my future, in fact I did it as soon as I finished with the exam,[2] and I have already had one lesson in Greek. My paper was prepared therefore without any restraint or restriction apart from the fact that I withheld the fact that I intend to practise what I have preached.[3]

It is not for me to say anything about the paper – all I shall say is this. The people who count at Charing Cross all liked it, while I myself was moved to an extent that I have never experienced before. I have visions of a great Wales in the future, Ieuan, and, God-willing I think that you and I will play a part in its coming. However, I must try to keep to the actual details for a while.

Mr Griffiths[4] informed me that he had got a *South Wales Daily News* representative there as he wanted my remarks to have a wider circulation than they had last year.[5] Feeling as I do that I had a real message for Wales I consented to his taking notes and further, when

[1] On 6 February 1925 ML-J had given an address to the Literary and Debating Society of his church at Charing Cross Road at which a reporter from this newspaper was present. His address, 'The Tragedy of Modern Wales', was given sensational treatment in this widely-read paper and he was strongly criticised as 'a young firebrand of twenty-five'.

[2] The diploma which made him a member of the Royal College of Physicians.

[3] The reference here is to his decision to turn from medicine to the work of the gospel ministry. With that in view he was studying Greek and he went to his denomination's Theological College at Aberystwyth to be interviewed as a prospective student the following month [March 1925]. After that interview he was not only uncertain as to the wisdom of going there but much pressure was put on him to remain in medicine. The outcome was, 'I made a solemn decision to go on with medicine'. *D. Martyn Lloyd-Jones: The First Forty Years 1899–1939,* Iain H. Murray (Edinburgh: Banner of Truth, 1982), p. 92.

[4] The Rev. Peter Hughes Griffiths, their minister.

[5] In March 1924 ML-J had spoken at the same meeting on 'The Signs of the Times'.

[5]

he came to me at the end and asked for my papers I gave them to him so that they might print what I actually said.

Well, next day they published the extracts which you have probably seen. There are numerous mistakes in it, for instance I said 'portals' and not 'pillars' of hell. Further than that, they have deliberately withheld most of my best sentences and phrases, in which I shewed that I was facing the problem from a Christian stand-point. I dealt at length in my introduction with that point and explained my attitude fully. When you see my paper you will understand how they have deliberately misrepresented what I said, just for the sake of creating a sensation. The London Editor wrote to me asking for permission to give a full publication, but so far they have not done so. If they are honest men they will not hesitate about it. However, I am not worrying at all, because I know that all the people whose opinion I value will understand what I meant. Given even the misrepresentation that has occurred I still think it may do some good. In any case, I have not yet finished with the Tragedy of Modern Wales.

At Charing Cross on Friday, the paper was received extraordinarily well, better than I had anticipated, for I really felt that it did not do justice to my theme and was in any case necessarily incomplete. The whole of my future life will be devoted to its completion and then I shall not have finished.

The criticisms that appeared in yesterday's paper have naturally served to strengthen my belief in what I have done and what I propose to do. Oh that I could see you now and talk to you for several hours. I thought of you several times this evening while I was with Bethan. I really think that she is now about as determined about Wales as I am – Ieuan, she almost makes a vital difference to me and yet when she asked me the other day whether she or Wales came first, I had to say that Wales came first. That was certainly the most awful question I have yet been asked during my life. She was great enough to say that she thought still more of me for saying that.

I am now longing for the time to come so that I may start on the way. The beginning which I had intended to be quiet and unobtrusive has, to say the least, been dramatic, hasn't it? It was the very last thing I wished for – but there you are, I have sufficient faith to believe that it is all for the best. They can heap all the personal abuse they like on me, it will make no difference, but I will not tolerate any misrepresentation of the truth.

I am deeply conscious of the great responsibility that now rests upon me and will rest upon me in the future, to maintain with undiminished energy and vigour, the work which I have begun. At this time, Ieuan, I look to your fellowship and friendship with a love and a longing greater than anything I have ever felt before. I often get glimpses of the future in which I always see us both together. Our friendship, my dear Ieuan, has been meant for some great purpose, that is why it has stood the strain of the past few years. Indeed, our fellowship has been that of those who believe in Him – our work in life should be to shew ourselves worthy of it. As I said on Friday night, I believe that conditions in Wales will have to become still worse before the great dawn appears. That intervening period will be our most trying time, but with faith and love we will be patient, and, when the time comes, let us pray that we shall be ready for it.

We shall have a hard struggle – all the resources of hell will be against us, but, if I mistake not, and the last few days have given me some experience of it, the effect of the persecution will be to make us feel that what we are now prepared to live for, we shall then be prepared to die for.

Is it not a glorious thing to be able to feel that we are fighting in the Great Cause, in the Great Crusade and that ultimately we shall triumph? We have had some never-to-be-forgotten times together in the past, but they will all be as nothing compared with what is in store for us.

Let us pray for one another, still more than we have ever done in the past.

Oh! how I would like to see you; but we must be patient, the time will soon come. I cannot help feeling that we are on the threshold of great things in the history of Wales – let us be worthy of the trust that has been invested in us.

I must now end with a request. Would you be kind enough to send to the hospital some of the papers that have been set in the first paper in Greek, in the entrance examination? The man who is coaching me would like to see them.

Good night, Ieuan, and may He who has guarded you and blessed you until this moment, be with you for ever. With fondest love from my mother and myself.

I remain,

Yours, in His love,

Martyn

Commitment to Preaching and his Engagement

7 Regency Street,
Westminster, London S.W.
16 June, 1926

[To Mr Ieuan Phillips]

My dear Ieuan,

At last I am keeping my promise – the promise I made the day the General Strike ended.

I need not assure you that I have since thought of you daily and longed for your society and your encouragement. For I have indeed passed through trying, not to say crushing experiences. I have been tried to the very marrow but, thank God, I still stand where I have always stood and my faith remains unshaken and unconquerable.[1]

You must have gathered from my last letter that great developments were about to take place. I gave you all details as I well knew that your knowledge of me and of my circumstances would enable you to fill in all the blanks. I therefore merely write to tell you how happy I was, and to let you know that I was prepared and preparing for whatever might happen, full of hope and of faith.

Ieuan bach, I thank God constantly for your love and for your faith. It means more to me than you can ever know.

---

[1] After a year of great personal turmoil, which he called 'a very great struggle', during which he lost over twenty pounds in weight, ML-J had recently reversed his decision to stay in medicine.

Bethan and I were talking about you yesterday and our experiences were identical. We both felt that merely to write to you was in a sense useless, that what we desired was to talk to you for hours and hours – on into the middle of the night, even unto the breaking of the dawn. There are certain stories that improve as they go on, the hours add to them and when so many hours have gone time suddenly ceases to exist and we are in that eternity known only to souls in communion with God. You know what I mean – we have had such occasions and we have both always felt greater after them, have we not?

Well, we must wait until we next meet, then we shall commune and who knows but that we shall rise from our chairs with a new vision, a new hope, yes, even as new men, and nothing will ever be the same again.

I have been more conscious of the hand of God during the last month than I have ever been before – we count, Ieuan, and count tremendously. Nothing is trivial, nothing is unimportant, everything matters and matters vitally. There is no responsibility except within the Kingdom. Bethan is writing to tell you about our intentions. We are going to get married.[1] That really does not express what is going to happen but you know all that I want to say and somehow cannot.

I know that I am beyond a doubt the luckiest man on the face of the earth at the present moment. It will make no difference to you and me. Being already your brother, that I shall soon be your brother-in-law makes no difference, and yet, as you know, it makes all the difference! I want to preach more than ever and am determined to preach. The precise nature of my future activities remains to be settled, but nothing can or will prevent my going about to tell people of 'the good news'.

I spent a very happy afternoon at Harrow yesterday and I am going there to have a long talk with your father on Saturday. I am

[1] Bethan Phillips, already qualified in medicine, had obtained her Bachelor of Surgery, the week before this letter was written. Formal parental approval of their engagement was not actually obtained until two days after this letter carried the news to Ieuan.

indeed overwhelmed with the love and the kindness of your father and mother.

Our partnership is about to commence, Ieuan – let the forces of hell beware!

I shall write again soon to let you know all developments.

My mother and Vincent are well, and as I have told you, I am truly proud of them.

But I still need your prayers, Ieuan.

With all my love,

I am, your brother,

      Martyn

Invitation to Sandfields, Aberavon

St Bartholomew's Hospital,
London E.C.1
13 November, 1926

[To Mr E. T. Rees][1]

Dear Mr Rees,

Thank you very much for your kindness in sending me these further particulars of the work etc. at Sandfields. As far as I can tell, it is precisely the kind of work that I have been longing to do for years.

---

[1] Mr E. T. Rees (1890–1985) was the secretary of Bethlehem Forward Movement Mission at Sandfields, Aberavon, in South Wales. In the summer of 1926 ML-J had become a candidate for the ministry of his denomination, with the approval of the London Presbytery gained in the early autumn. But instead of proceeding to formal training, ML-J took the very unexpected course of applying for a post in his denomination's home mission arm, the 'Forward Movement'. His heart was set on evangelism among the unchurched in Wales and had the way not opened for him in the Forward Movement he thought of the Salvation Army. A letter from E. T. Rees early in November asked him to preach at the Sandfields Mission on 28 November 1926. This was accepted at once in a letter of 8 November in which ML-J asked for more details of the work. This further letter, though prior to his first visit, almost assumes the beginning of the long-term relationship which was to follow.

I am eagerly looking forward to the 28th when I shall have the pleasure of meeting you and all the friends at Sandfields. I know from your letters that we shall get on well together and under Divine guidance that we shall do all we can together in a spirit of love and comradeship to fight the forces of evil.

The Rev. R. J. Rees,[1] whom I saw on Friday, spoke so highly of you that I feel it will be a real privilege if I am allowed to work in conjunction with you.

I shall let you know next week as to the time of arrival of my train on Saturday the 27th etc.

If there is anything concerning me which you would like to know, please write and ask me.

Again thanking you and with all good wishes and greetings,

I remain,

Yours sincerely,

D. M. Lloyd-Jones

Anticipation of First Visit to Sandfields

St Bartholomew's Hospital,
London E.C.1
25 November [1926]

[To Mr E. T. Rees]

Dear Mr Rees,

As promised, I am writing to let you know the time of my arrival on Saturday. I shall leave Paddington with the 1.18 p.m. which gets me to Port Talbot at 5.27 p.m.

I need scarcely add that I am looking forward to meeting you and all the friends at Sandfields with eagerness and pleasant anticipation.

Your last letter has been a great source of joy to me and has strengthened me in all my various decisions. I am one of those who

---

[1] Superintendent of the Forward Movement whom ML-J had first contacted in June.

believes that honest and sincere work for the kingdom can never fail. However depressing the state of religion may be at the present time, I have a profound conviction that a time is coming, and coming soon, when the truth shall prevail and men and women will come to the cross.

Until Saturday then and with all good wishes,

I am,

Yours sincerely,

D. M. Lloyd-Jones

Hope for the Future and Plans for a Second Visit

St Bartholomew's Hospital,
London E.C.1
6 December [1926]

[To Mr E. T. Rees]

My Dear Mr Rees,

Once more I have to thank you for numerous kindnesses.

First of all, let me thank you most sincerely for your delightful letter of the other day and for your much appreciated present. I have read the book and, as you anticipated, I enjoyed it immensely. As you remarked, it sums up our philosophy completely.

I feel somewhat ashamed of myself for not having written to you and Mrs Rees to thank you for your great kindness to me while I stayed with you. As I told you, I am a very poor correspondent at the best of times moreover, I comforted myself with the thought that you must have realised how greatly I was enjoying myself. Whatever else may happen after my arrival at Aberavon, one thing is certain and that is that you and I will be great friends, and as I have assured you time and again, I am looking forward to our work together with great eagerness.[1]

---

[1] Although nothing had been formally determined at this date, ML-J's own mind on his future with the people at Sandfields was clearly made up on his first visit.

Your letter of this morning has naturally filled me with joy and hope. Of course, I realise fully the seriousness of the commission which I am taking up, but it is a high adventure and a crusade of hope.

Whatever may happen, our cause must triumph, and if we fail (which God forbid) what we stand for will still go on and will in the end prove supreme. That is the spirit in which I am taking up the task, realising that human endeavour at its highest is only feeble and that our only hope is that we shall be given of the Holy Spirit freely. Of course, I am looking forward to all the various details which you will have to give to me when we meet. With regard to the hospitality problem, I have discussed the matter with Miss Phillips and she feels that she would prefer to stay with Mrs Robson. She is writing to Mrs Robson now to confirm the arrangements I made and to state the time of our arrival etc. With regard to myself, I hardly know what to say. Of course, there is no question as to where I should like to be and you know where that is. But I do not believe in keeping the willing 'horse' working and therefore I feel that the only thing I can say is this, that I leave it to you to make any arrangements that you may choose. I shall be perfectly happy wherever I am, but like most other men, I have my preferences.

Perhaps you will be good enough to let me know what you decide so that I can write to Mr W. J. Williams. Miss Phillips and I shall leave Paddington at 5.55 p.m. and hope to reach Aberavon at 10.14 p.m. if all is well. We shall take some supper on the train so please do not allow anyone to prepare a meal for us that night.

I think these are all the points I can think of now.

I am looking forward to seeing you. How are Mrs Rees and the little girl? My very best wishes to the three of you, in which Miss Phillips joins me.

Yours very sincerely,

    D. M. Lloyd-Jones

Acceptance of the Call to Sandfields

St Bartholomew's Hospital,
London E.C.1
22 December, 1926

[To Mr E. T. Rees]
Dear Mr Rees,

May I thank you, on behalf of The Bethlehem Forward Movement Church at Sandfields, Aberavon, for the great honour the Church has done me by asking me to become its pastor.

It is un-necessary for me to say that I readily and gladly accept the invitation, and deeply appreciate what a great privilege it will be to be allowed to work for the coming of the kingdom among my good friends at Sandfields. It is for us, by prayer and spiritual exercises, to prepare ourselves for the great work that lies ahead of us. Let us pray that we be given of His strength and that we be made new men and women worthy of the sacred trust that is being placed in our hands.

With heartiest greetings and all good wishes to you all as a Church,

I am,

Yours very truly,

D. M. Lloyd-Jones

Thoughts on his Summer Holiday

12 Vincent Square,
Westminster, London S.W.1
9 August, 1927

[To Mr E. T. Rees]
My dear E. T.,

I found your post-card here, waiting for me yesterday and was truly glad to see your writing once more. Yes, you must forgive me for not writing from Newcastle Emlyn. The country was so good and some friends were kind enough to take us about so much, that I just did nothing at all. My mother has been chastising me sorely for not writing to her.[1] You know that feeling that we get occasionally, particularly on holiday, in which one takes a kind of brutal delight in saying to oneself, 'Well now I'm on holiday and there is nothing that I *must* do.' It was something like that, that governed all my thoughts and actions last week. Please forgive me therefore!

I was very glad to find that you were comfortably settled at Ilfracombe. You really needed a rest badly. I often wonder how you manage to keep well in spite of all your activities – it must be that you have been blessed with a physique of unusual strength and resilience. It is all the more important therefore that you should look after it and preserve it. I have thought a lot about you during the past week and of all the things that have happened to us during the past six to eight months.

I feel we ought to thank God for having brought us together and for having given us the privilege of working together in the Great Cause.

I have a curious feeling these days which I have never experienced on any previous holiday – I somehow cannot relax and forget my work as I used to. The present seems an enforced pause prior to still greater effort. When I think of our little church in Sandfields, of the love and of the fellowship, and of those men who are standing on the doorstep, I feel that it is indeed a community that cannot be matched anywhere.

What a terrible place London is! My week-end at Llangeitho was extremely pleasant – in many ways never to be forgotten. The shoe-maker, who was away when the Brotherhood was there, had returned and was in his best form. Many complimentary remarks were passed concerning 'the nice men from Aberavon'. The main impression left was that exceptionally fine spirit was manifested as between the men themselves. What better impression could have been left?![2]

---

[1] They were now staying with his mother on this the first break since he had gone to Aberavon.

[2] Llangeitho was the home of ML-J's boyhood. For the 'shoemaker', and outings of the men of Sandfields to this historic spot in Calvinistic Methodist history, see *D. Martyn Lloyd-Jones: The First Forty Years*, pp. 12, 161–2.

Well, do enjoy yourself and have a good rest. Please think of us sometimes and remember that we are thinking of you.

With our love and all good wishes.

I remain,

Yours very sincerely,

Martyn

Thankfulness for the First Year

57 Victoria Road,
Aberavon, Port Talbot
7 February, 1928

[To Mr E. T. Rees]

My dear E. T. ,

I feel I must write you just a short note now before I rush off to Taibach. I had intended writing you a long letter but what with callers and visitors I have scarcely had a moment to myself. And yet, after all perhaps, there is no need of a lengthy letter. You know well what I would say to you.

I thought as I sat in the pulpit on Sunday night during the collection of all the things that have happened during the first year. I thanked God for all but, believe me when I say that above all I thanked him for you. I often try to picture what it would have been were you not the secretary here. Of one thing I shall always remain quite sure that what made me 'fall in love' with Sandfields when I came that first Saturday was the personality and character of him whom I had anticipated was at least a middle-aged man.

I am quite sure of that. That first surprise, filling my heart with joy as it did, and removing all sorts of obstacles and questionings, opened the way to all the things that followed.

I look back also on our friendship which is, to me, one of the greatest treasures of my life. We understand each other too deeply in a sense to say these things, but you have no idea of my true and deep admiration of you: your self-sacrifice for the cause, your constant devotion and encouragement in spite of all those little pin-pricks which you have to tolerate, amaze me more and more.

We are remarkably alike in many things and I know how you feel and suffer occasionally, but when I see you triumph and the smile re-appearing on your face, I wonder more and more. Your action in connection with this —— [indecipherable] has touched me very deeply. You are always showering these things on me and you never get any recognition whatsoever. You efface yourself and greatly over-estimate me.

All I can say is that you have become to me, a brother, one of whom I think almost exactly as I do of Vincent. My mother, I know, regards you almost as a son.

Is it not really wonderful? Especially when we realise that it is because we both love Him and find ourselves together at His feet.

I cannot express what I would like to say, but I know that whatever the future may have in store, we shall be found fighting together for the Cause by which we live. I shall not see you now until Friday. If you have the time do please come down and have a chat and some supper.

Our fond love to Mrs Rees, Linda and your good self.

Yours very sincerely,

Martyn

London or Wales?

28 Victoria Road,
Aberavon, Port Talbot
16 May, 1938

[To the Secretary of the South Wales Association
 of the Presbyterian Church of Wales][1]

Dear Brother,

I write to inform you (and through you the other five representatives of the Association whom I met at Neath together with you on April 6th, and through them the South Wales Association

---

[1] On 1 May 1938 ML-J had announced his resignation from the pastorate at Sandfields as from the end of July (see *D. Martyn Lloyd-Jones: The First Forty Years*, p. 337). This had led to widespread discussion within

[17]

which will meet at Llandeilo on June 14th) of the response which I have made to the appeal of the Association in the matter of 'the call', which I had received to the pastorate of the Marylebone Presbyterian Church, London.

My decision has been given publicity already in the religious press by the friends at Marylebone.

I write, therefore, not primarily to acquaint you with the fact that I have declined that invitation, but rather to express my feelings and sentiments with regard to the action of the Association in appointing the six representatives to meet me.

I say quite honestly and sincerely that the action came to me as a very great surprise, and that its main effect upon me has been to humble me and to fill me with a sense of my unworthiness. It would be affectation on my part to conceal the fact that I regard this as the highest tribute that has or ever can be paid me or any one else.

Nothing can be more precious than the thought that one has the affection and the trust of one's brethren.

As I indicated to the deputation, it was not my desire, nor indeed my intention, to leave the Connexion.

My consideration of 'the call' to Marylebone was dictated solely by physical causes and the desire to render to the Kingdom of God on earth the maximum amount of service of which I am capable.

The opening-out before me, therefore, by the brethren, of a field of service within the Connexion which is of the very first

---

his own denomination and beyond on what his future work would be. He had preached at Marylebone Presbyterian Church, London, on the first Sunday of 1938 and received a unanimous call to its pulpit. This was not the first attempt of a London congregation to draw him to the capital. Islington Chapel had approached him in 1933, urged by Dr J. D. Jones, one of the leaders of English Congregationalism. This letter was first printed in the *Agenda of the Quarterly Association of the Presbyterian Church of Wales to be held at Salem, Llandeilo, June 14–16, 1938,* pp. 36–37.

importance, immediately decided my course of action.[1]

I informed the friends at Marylebone of my decision and of the reasons which dictated it.

It is but right and just that I should say that I fully realise that the six brethren whom I met had no power to commit the Association to anything definite, and that I have acted solely and entirely on their personal pledges and on my estimate of them as leaders within the denomination.

I should like to place on record my deep sense of gratitude to them for their courtesy and their kindness, and for their overgenerous estimate of my performances in the past and of my possible services in the future.

I thus leave myself in the hands of the brethren, assuring them of my love in Christ Jesus and of my determination to labour and to strive 'according to his working which worketh in me mightily', so never to betray their confidence and their trust.

With warmest greetings,

Your brother and fellow-labourer,

D. Martyn Lloyd-Jones

Eleven-Years Friendship

Rhyl,
30 July, 1938

[To Mr E. T. Rees]

My dear E. T.,

As promised in my note last Wednesday I am writing a few words. Under separate cover (as the authorities say) you will receive something which I ask you to accept with my love and my deepest gratitude for all you have been and all you have done

---

[1] It was urged upon him that the principalship of the denomination's theological college at Bala would most probably soon be vacant and he was eminently suited for that post.

during the past eleven and a half years. It was my intention to do this before we left Aberavon. My failure to do so was not due to the inevitable rush and hurry of packing and farewelling etc. It was rather due to the fact that I simply could not decide as to the form which my small token of gratitude to you should take. Even now I am not fully satisfied. But I felt that I must decide without further delay, and feeling strongly as I did that the token I gave must be something personal, i.e. something you could carry about with you, I decided upon this fountain-pen. I do hope that it will please you and that it will be of some use to you. If the nib is not the precise one that you like I am assured that Messrs W. H. Smith at Port Talbot will change it for you.

I could say much, but in a sense I told you everything when I told you that you were undoubtedly the most vital human factor in my ever going to Sandfields. And throughout the years you have ever been the same.

I find it quite impossible still to realise that we have left and that I am no longer the minister of Sandfields, Aberavon. But I know that as the months and the years, God willing, shall pass, I shall be ever more and more grateful for all the help and the friendship, indeed the love I received from you.

What the future holds we do not know, but it cannot possibly be happier than the past years.

Accept my deepest thanks then for all and may God continue to bless you and Mrs Rees and Linda and Roger even as He has done.

We all join in warmest love to you all.

Yours ever sincerely,

Martyn

P.S. We go to Talybont on Tuesday. Remember your promise to visit us there – and in your new car! We are enjoying the rest very much. My eye has healed once more. M.

Gratitude for Encouragement

12 Vincent Square,
Westminster, London S.W.1
11 September, 1939

[To the Moderator of the South Wales Association][1]
My Dear Brother,

Will you kindly convey to the South Wales Association meeting at Trinity, Swansea, on September 13th my profound gratitude for the message of goodwill and encouragement that was sent to me from the last meeting of the Association held at Conwil. Were it not for the troubled and anxious days through which we are passing, I should be tempted to acknowledge the message at greater length.[2] But pressed as you will be for time to transact other and more important business, I shall content myself with saying I have been deeply moved and humbled by this signal manifestation of what I cannot but regard as the love, as well as the confidence of the denomination of which I am still proud to call myself a member.

What the future holds I do not know, but whatever it may be, it can never be a time of greater happiness than that which I spent as fellow labourer with my brethren in South Wales.

I shall strive to be worthy of the good opinion of the Association by being always a good minister of Jesus Christ.

May He bless us all and grant us special grace to proclaim His Holy Name in this dark and difficult hour.

My love in Christ to you all,
Yours very sincerely,
D. M. Lloyd-Jones

[1] The hopes of brethren in the South Wales Association that ML-J would be appointed to the Bala College were not fulfilled and in April 1939 he had accepted the call of Westminster Chapel, London, to serve as co-pastor with Dr G. Campbell Morgan from September. See notes below on pp. 39–41.

[2] World War II had begun on 3 September 1939.

2

TO HIS WIFE

Second Visit to North America[1]

RMS 'Berengaria'
13 May, 1937

My Dear Bethan, Elizabeth and Ann,

I have just had my tea, and have also just received your telegram, and the one from the 'Neathites.'[2] I must confess that your telegram was almost too much for me and made my heart long for you all.

Here I am writing in my own room, and nobody with me. Harcombe will have told you that Mr Butler moved me from B 262 to B 192, and I gave him a shilling for doing so. This is an excellent room with two beds in it. Since there was no other passenger wanting it, I have it all at my service! Compared with the 'Olympic'[3] I am in real luxury. I have also a table to write on so I need not go to the writing room at all. Mr Butler came to see

---

[1] This was virtually his first visit to the United States as, apart from five days at Chautauqua and an overnight train journey to New York for departure, the nine weeks of the summer of 1932 had been spent in Canada. Bethan and Elizabeth had been with him on that occasion but at this date Ann was only a baby of five months, and so for the period of his absence the family went to stay with Mrs Lloyd-Jones' parents in the family home at Harrow.

[2] 'Neathites' – Mrs Lloyd-Jones' brother, the Rev. Ieuan Phillips, and his family, who served a congregation at Neath, close to Dr Lloyd-Jones' own at Sandfields, Aberavon.

[3] The vessel which had taken them to Canada in 1932.

me – he is a thoroughly nice man. He took me to the chief
steward, a man called 'Jones', but he did not understand Welsh. I
was also introduced to the Purser, so I hope for good treatment
from them.

I was very glad indeed that you did not come to Southampton.
It began to rain and everything looked very dreary. I'm afraid I
could never have borne to leave you behind there. I must say
you were a very good girl at Waterloo.[1] I was afraid to look at
you, in case I caused a scene! How I arranged to make this trip, I
do not know. But I must not start on that tack or I shall be too
unhappy to bear the circumstances at all. I am determined to
make the best of it now, hoping that that will make the time go
more quickly. But, Bethan, dear, you are dearer to me than
ever and I feel prouder of you than ever before. I hope that this
change will do you, all three, good. God has been marvellously
good to me – you, Elizabeth and Ann, and haven't we been blessed
with two exceptionally sweet little girls. You will all be in my
thoughts every step of this trip and I shall be daily thanking God
for you.

There is no kind of news yet, of course. We hope to reach
Cherbourg about 8.00–8.30 tonight. Oh! that you were here with
me. Look after yourselves and be happy. Strange to think that
my next chance of sending you a letter will be from the USA. All,
all my love to you, my three beloved ones, and especially to the
biggest of them.

Ever, always yours,
Martyn

Warmest greetings to all there.
Forgive this poor letter, I can't write today.
All my love, M.

[1] The London railway station from which the boat train left for
Southampton.

News from Pittsburgh

Pittsburgh,
23 May, 1937[1]

My Dear Bethan,

Here I am trying to get a word written to you, before the evening service. These people are keeping me so busy that there is no time even to think. I was truly glad to get your letter in New York on Friday morning, before leaving, and also Elizabeth's letter. I had not expected to hear from you as soon as that, and so it was a pleasant surprise, in the true meaning of the term. Seeing your handwriting on the envelope was almost enough in itself. Back to English now,[2] in order to save time and also to make things easier for us both. I believe, too, that the historical style is the most suitable for giving the news. I told you, in my letter posted on Wednesday night, that we both stayed the night at the Allisons's.[3] They have a nice house and Mr Allison is an exceptionally nice man. She is rather overpowering! I think mother will be happy and comfortable there. Mr Allison took me into New York on Thursday morning. I said Goodbye to mother before leaving. Pugh[4] met us and we spent the rest of the day getting my voucher for travelling and fixing up my journey etc. I felt that I knew New York well, and could easily have got about myself. There are just one or two new things. We had very heavy rain several times

---

[1] Between this letter and the last, there was a long letter on 18 May which is printed in *D. Martyn Lloyd-Jones: The Fight of Faith 1939–1981*, Iain H. Murray (Edinburgh: Banner of Truth, 1990), pp. 781–84.

[2] The first part of the letter, as was common in letters to his wife, was written in Welsh. The closing paragraphs of these letters were also in Welsh and Mrs Lloyd-Jones, to whom we owe the translation, may have found some difficulty in finding English equivalents for some of his words.

[3] 'We' is a reference to his mother who had travelled with him and was making the journey primarily to visit her brother.

[4] Fellow-countryman, the Rev. Dr E. Cynolwyn Pugh who served a congregation in New York.

[27]

during the day. That night I went to the 'Seiat' at Pugh's Chapel. It is strongly reminiscent of Charing Cross[1] in every respect. I spent the night with them. They live in a flat. They did their best to make me comfortable and happy. On our travels we went inside the Fifth Avenue Church.[2] Having seen it, I was rather sorry I had refused to take the afternoon meeting that had been arranged for me there on June 6th. It is easily the nicest chapel I have seen on this continent as yet. However, it is probably all for the best.

I left New York on the 11.00 a.m. train on Friday morning, Pugh seeing me off. I was in a parlour car and really comfortable. The nine-and-a-half hours' journey was particularly enjoyable. I had intended reading a lot, but the scenery was so excellent that I scarcely read at all. We saw nothing in any way like it in Canada – it is really entrancingly beautiful. For the first three hours it was rich agricultural land. From then on, wonderful forest and mountain scenery, following a great river almost to its source. Oh! how I longed and longed that you had been with me. You may think me foolish, but I pictured, time and time again, you coming with me sometime on this journey in the future! So, get ready! I would so like you to see it. I can't hope to describe it. I just looked and looked at it the whole way and did not get tired at all. Fortunately for me, the High Sheriff of the county was travelling with me, and, realising that I was a stranger, explained everything to me. I had three meals on the train. In due course I arrived at Pittsburgh, having passed through Newark, Philadelphia, Harrisburg etc., etc. My host here, Mr J. R. Jones, was meeting me at the station. I could have recognised him easily from his brother, the Vicar of St. Mary's. He is a very much better looking edition of the same thing. He is a delightful little man, and so is his wife! They have a lovely little home of the same type exactly as that of the Richard Roberts's.[3] If anything it is nicer. I felt at home

[1] The Calvinistic Methodist chapel in London to which ML-J and his wife had both belonged.

[2] Presbyterian church opened in 1875, during the ministry of John Hall, the congregation having been built up at Nineteenth Street under the ministry of J. W. Alexander.

[3] Their hosts in Toronto in 1932.

at once and have done so ever since. I have a lovely room and a comfortable bed. I only wish that I was staying here right through.

Yesterday they drove me down to the city, and there I meet Dr Klein, who, as you know, is arranging all for me out here.[1] He is a delightful man in every respect and is anxious to do all he can for me. He and I were then motored by my host all round the city. This is a great place, and totally unlike Toronto. It is a series of hills, and also the junction of two rivers that go to form the Ohio river. It is a great city – the place where Carnegie made his fortune, and also the Mellows. It was once thronged with Welsh people in the days when nearly all the steel industry was here. There are not so many here today. Some of the buildings are mills. The show piece is the university, which is called 'the Cathedral of learning'. It is the only university in the world which is all in one building. The other show piece is the church in which I preached this morning and where I am due tonight again. It is the finest non-conformist church probably in the world. That is no exaggeration. It was built by the Mellows in memory of their mother, and cost at least £1,000,000! If you entered it without knowing, you would swear you were in a cathedral. I shall be bringing with me the book which tells you all about it, so you will see for yourself. I went in yesterday afternoon just to try the pulpit etc. There are three ministers, a large paid choir, and it takes £25,000 a year to run it. It is really quite unbelievable. I have certainly never seen anything like it.

24 May '37. I began to feel too fatigued to go on any further at that point, so I am resuming today. After we had finished all the round of sight-seeing, it was already 4.30 p.m. I then slept for about an hour. On waking, I discovered that the leading Welshman of the town had arranged a dinner, in my honour, for 6.30 p.m.! It

---

[1] Dr William Klein had invited him to the United States on behalf of the League of Faith, an organisation intended to rally conservatives within the Presbyterian Church in the USA. Clarence Macartney, President of the League of Faith, was minister of the First Presbyterian Church of Pittsburgh. Further information on this visit will be found in *D. Martyn Lloyd-Jones: The First Forty Years*, pp. 327–30.

was very nice and a very interesting gathering. The Welsh here are
a very fine type, and they account for what is best in the city. They
all spoke, and I said a few words at the close. They seemed to come
from all parts of Wales. After that, I confess that I was rather tired.
I did not sleep too well that night, largely, I think, owing to some
orange juice in an ice which I ate! Yesterday was a strenuous day.
In the morning at the East Liberty Church, the building was
practically full, which means about 1300–1500 people. I will not
attempt to describe the service etc., as it would take too much
time. The other ministers gave me a very warm welcome, and all I
had to do was preach. The procession into the church put the
Sherborne Street[1] one into the shade. I shall tell you all about it. I
preached on I Peter 2:7, and found considerable freedom in doing
so. The system of microphones made the speaking really easy, in
spite of the building. I had to shake hands and speak to a large
number at the close, and found, as at Toronto, a real thirst for the
Gospel.

In the afternoon I was due at Dr Clarence Macartney's church –
cousin of Mr Robertson of Toronto. He is a peculiar man – dour
and almost prohibiting. Mel Trotter had warned me to expect that,
adding that beneath it all he was a very good fellow – a hard-baked
bachelor. Dr Louis Evans, a son of Dr William Evans, who you
remember was in England a few years ago, was my chairman, and
other prominent ministers were present. Dr Macartney prayed.
There was an exceptionally large congregation for an afternoon
meeting. I preached on 'Dorcas'. The building was not too good,
and I felt that the service was not a good one, but at the close, Dr
Evans, and the secretary of the National Board of Missions, and Dr
Klein came to me begging of me to give that message again at
Columbus. Dr Macartney was also pleased and gave me a copy of
his latest book. He is a little like Robertson in appearance, but
nothing like so pleasant. There were large numbers of Welsh
people at the service. Last night again, we had a good congregation at the East Liberty Church, and I preached on Matthew

---

[1] The Toronto church he had supplied in 1932. A procession into a
service was unknown to British nonconformity.

7:13, 14. That was easily the best service of the day. In spite of the three services and the fact that I had not preached for a fortnight, I had practically no trouble at all with my voice. I felt again that the people were just longing for the Gospel. The chief minister there is an exceptionally nice man. I have already had numerous invitations to return here again for preaching. Dr Evans was most anxious that I should promise to come and to preach each night for a week under the auspices of all the churches. A happy crowd was here last night, until about midnight. I slept very well after it all. I am leaving for Columbus on the 2.55 p.m. train, and should be there, of course, until Friday morning – including Dayton. I shall write to you from there, D.V., on Wednesday and Thursday giving you an account of the conference. The plan, then, is for me to return here. Then I shall be motored over the Allegheny Mountains, and catch the train for Utica the other side. I am told that that is one of the best bits of scenery in the whole of the States – a 200 mile drive.

There is one constant regret right through everything – that you are not with me. I was counting it out in bed this morning, that by three weeks today, I ought to be with you again. You said in your letter that you hoped I would not forget you – I am prepared to enter into a competition with you on that score without the slightest hesitation! I hope you three are all right and enjoying yourselves. How are Elizabeth and Ann? I expect I shall see a very great change in the latter.

Well, now I must get going and pack my bag. By the way, Mr Allison gave me the loan of an attaché case, so the only luggage I now have is the Williams's bag and the attaché. This makes things very easy for me. As I said earlier, I hope to write again on Wednesday, when I finish speaking in Columbus. Oh! that I could speak to you on the phone, just to hear your voice but I must live on patience for three weeks yet.

All my love to you, dearest girl in the world. There is no one like you anywhere. The more I see of others the more obvious does this become. Kiss each of the girls for me.

Yours for ever and ever,

    Martyn

The Pre-Assembly Conference, Columbus, Ohio

Deshler-Wallick Hotel,
Columbus, Ohio
26 May, 1937

My Dear Bethan,

Well, here I am, having finished the work in Columbus, Ohio, enjoying a spot of relaxation to write to you once more. As you see from this notepaper, I am staying in a big hotel, like all the others who have come to this Conference. I have not had a letter from you since I left New York, but I have just realised that letters take an extra two days to arrive here. I felt very homesick on Monday. With me on the train was Dr Wilson from New York. I had met him on Sunday afternoon. In the Pullman he met another minister and his wife. After talking for a while, Dr Wilson said to the other minister's wife: 'You know, you make me feel very homesick for my wife – I think I'll send a card to her to come along.' 'Yes do,' said the other, 'most of the wives are coming this time.' And me, having to think of the dearest little wife in the world, thousands of miles away, across the sea! I became totally depressed as I thought of it. When we arrived here, I saw that the wives were here by the dozen! This is surely one of the best hotels in the world. I never saw anything like it. I have a double-bedded room with a private bathroom, toilet etc. This is real luxury, but Oh! the bed is much too big for one! You ought to be here with me.

Columbus is a very beautiful city, of some 250,000 inhabitants, and marvellous buildings. I slept very badly on Monday night. It seems to me that the reason for this was that I was over-tired after the Sunday, and all the travelling, and, also the terrific heat has come suddenly. When I awoke yesterday morning I had a severe headache – the same type exactly as I had last year when I failed to go to Llantwit Major. The tea at breakfast time made no difference, and there I was, facing a day when I was to speak three times.[1] As I

[1] He was in Columbus for a two-day pre-Assembly Conference on Evangelism, being the main engagement for which the League of Faith had invited him.

was going to the first meeting, I met Dr Hutchison, the minister of
the church where I preached in Pittsburgh. I told him how I felt. I
had severe tachycardia[1], indeed I was in real anxiety. I had not
written a word of what I intended to say, and I felt that I could not
put the thoughts I had into any kind of order. There were two
others speaking before me, with written out papers before them.
Well, as they spoke I felt that they did not have much 'form', but
were just saying things in rather a monotonous way. This did me
the world of good. My text – as you saw in the programme – was:
'The Present Situation, Analysis and Investigation'. After speaking
for two minutes I felt that I had hold of myself and of the people,
and I spoke for forty minutes. I told them quite plainly the reason
for the state of church today was the substitution of philosophy for
Biblical Theology, and I worked that point out. I have never been
so thankful for the consistent reading which has been my custom
for the past ten years. I had a feeling, as I was giving a review of
the history of the past century, that I was telling them things that
they knew nothing of before. The note-books were out, all over
the place – indeed, it nearly made me feel I was giving a lecture. I
finished by showing that humanism and psychology and all such
things were a failure, and that there was only one thing to do –
return to the Bible.[2] I saw that the address was having a visible
influence, and at the end so many people came to speak to me that
I thought I should never leave the chapel. One minister came to
speak to me from Texas – right down in the South – and said: 'I
would gladly travel the thousands of miles from Texas many times
over, just to hear that.' Dr Macartney came to me and said: 'You
have no idea of what that address means, and what it will accom-
plish.' And so it went on right through lunch time. My headache
was all right while I was speaking, but afterwards as bad as ever.

1 'Tachycardia' – rapid pulse.
2 Commenting on ML-J's speaking, *The Presbyterian* (3 June 1937) said:
'He won followers and provoked enmity, but this time the enmity was on
the part of noted theological indifferentists and religious Liberals. Dr
Lloyd-Jones laid down Christian truth and called to repentance on lines
that were so forthright and particular, that some of his audience felt
uneasy.'

In the afternoon, the man who organised the preaching mission that was held here last winter, was speaking before me for half-an-hour, a typical official type whose work was to organise this and that. Speaking after him, I preached on 1 Cor. 12:27. I wonder whether you remember that sermon, and the description I have in it of 'spiritual convulsions'? It had a very powerful influence. Poor old Cynolwyn felt it was one of the best things he had ever heard. It really was an outstanding service and I spoke plainly to them. The first man to jump up on to the platform was Dr Hutchison, Pittsburgh, and this is what he said to me: 'Tell me, how do you get that headache?' That sermon made a deep impression on a group of young ministers. They came to me at the end, and last night we had a long chat. I am due to meet them again tonight. Last night, at 8.45, in the Memorial Hall, I preached on Isaac. I had no trouble at all with my voice. It was a good service, and yet, it was the afternoon sermon that had gripped the ministers mostly. The minister of the largest church in Detroit came to me and said: 'Your visit will make history – you have demonstrated that there is no incompatibility between a first-rate intellect and evangelism.' In each of these meetings there was a public plea for me to return soon.

This morning I was following Dr Robert E. Speer, the man that poor Machen made an attack upon.[1] He spoke well and in an excellent spirit. He is now seventy, and is retiring from his work as

---

[1] J. G. Machen (1881–1937), principal founder of Westminster Theological Seminary and leader of an unsuccessful reform movement within the Presbyterian Church in the USA. He had charged the Foreign Missions Board of the denomination (of which Speer and C. B. McAfee were the secretaries) with tolerating liberal candidates for the foreign mission field. At this date ML-J had not thoroughly looked at the issues. The reasons for Machen's criticism of Speer are clearly given in J. G. Machen, *Modernism and the Board of Foreign Missions of the Presbyterian Church in the USA,* (1933), pp. 57–64. Machen had been suspended from the ministry of this denomination at the General Assembly which had met twelve months before the League of Faith brought ML-J to Columbus. The League's hopes of rallying conservative strength were not to succeed.

secretary of the Board of Foreign Missions, this year. To me, he seemed perfectly sound. He said: 'I sum up my faith in these words – "My hope is built on nothing less, Than Jesu's blood and right-eousness".' I preached on Romans 1:14. In my opinion this was the best service of all. Well, it is very obvious to me that these people are thirsting for the truth. Dozens and dozens of ministers from all parts of the country have come to me, to express their thanks, to ask questions, and to say they were going home to begin preaching in a new way, to confess that they have been 'off the track', etc. If I were to accept all the invitations received, I would have to live in this country! They are aware of their bankruptcy. You shall have further details again.

Naturally, I do feel somewhat tired, but not too bad. The heat is over-powering. I intend to have a bath tonight! I am going to Dayton for tomorrow night, after tea, by car, and returning here after the service. I shall be leaving by the 8.00 a.m. train on Friday morning. I shall try to write again on Sunday. I shall be travelling all day Friday and Saturday. If I have the opportunity, I will try to write a letter to Ieuan that he can read in Sandfields. But do write to him and tell him to say that the work, and the heat, and the travelling, together, make writing very difficult but that I promise to tell them the complete story when I return.

How are you my three dear ones, I wonder. I would give all the world for you to be here with me. If ever the two of us come again to this country, I am determined that we shall have a second honey-moon in this hotel, come what may! I am sending Elizabeth a P.C. I must try to get some P.C.s of this place to send to some of the friends, e.g. Lloyd-Jenkins of Aberystwyth, etc. But truly I have never been busier. I cannot walk through this place without people coming to speak to me. A fortnight today I'll be leaving New York. Half the time has nearly gone and then I'll be home with you.

Well, my dear, dear love, the best wife and girl in all the world, receive every bit of my love,

Ever yours,

Martyn

The General Assembly and his Journeys

En Route to Scranton,
1 June, 1937

My Dear Bethan,

I had meant to write to you yesterday morning, but it happened to be a grand holiday here – one that is called 'Remembrance Day'. So there was no post going out at all, and, on top of that, they had arranged to take us up country, to see the lakes. In view of all this, I am afraid that this will be a very scrappy letter. The heat today is worse than ever – the hottest day this year. I'll try to continue my report from where I left off in my last letter. Back to English for the 'report'.

The remainder of Wednesday last week was spent in talking to people and having discussions etc. On Thursday, the Assembly proper opened. I was not at all impressed. I felt that they lacked dignity and the real spirit of religion. Moreover, the 'machine' was much in evidence and it was clear that the moderatorial election had been fully arranged beforehand. It was after writing to you that the request came, and that most urgently, that I should return again for the next year. Next year's Assembly happens to be the 150th and is to be held in Philadelphia. They were most insistent and they are preparing to renew the attack when I get to New York. I shall not go of course! After tea on Thursday, we were motored to Dayton – 70 miles. Dayton is famous for aeroplanes, frigidaire machines, and cash registers. The chapel, again, was of the cathedral type and very difficult to speak in. I preached on John 8:32, feeling that it was what they needed. It certainly made them sit up and look up. We had a terrible thunderstorm while there. We did not reach Columbus until 12.40 a.m. By when I had packed my goods it was 1.30 a.m. I slept well, but had to get up at 7.10 to catch the 8.00 a.m. train. I succeeded. Cynolwyn Pugh came with me to the station. He is a very kind man, and, if he were only a little less ambitious, would be much more successful.

I reached Pittsburgh at 1.55 p.m. and, after about half-an-hour, the daughter and son-in-law of Dr J. R. Jones and I started upon our motor drive over the Allegheny Mountains. We did 234 miles altogether. I dislike motoring more than ever. I had a bad head-ache and felt sick at times, but I managed to get through without trouble. The scenery was certainly wonderful. The highest point we touched was practically 3,000 ft. above sea level. The one thing that spoilt everything was that you were not with me. You would have enjoyed the scenery very much. It was endless in its majesty. Dai Pearce's word 'panorama' is the only one that can truly describe it.[1] It was to me the most unexpected pleasure to find that we were going through Gettysburg. I saw the place where Abraham Lincoln delivered the famous speech, and saw something of the battlefield. I am sending E. some pictures of it. I could not help thinking of my father and how delighted he would have been to have visited that place. He made a special journey to take off his hat to the statue of Lincoln opposite Westminster Abbey, when it was unveiled. I bought a little booklet which gives an account of the battle. I slept the night at the house of the father and mother of my driver/host, at a place called Columbia. Their name is Reinhart – German, Dutch. Mr Reinhart's father was one of the Moravian Brethren. On Saturday I left Columbia at 11.15 a.m., travelled to New York, changed stations there, and set off again for Utica, arriving there at 8.55 p.m. We did that actual journey that night, on our way to New York. The scenery was excellent. It is a great pity that we missed it. I thought much of that night. R. R. Williams and two other men met me at the station. On being asked whether I preferred to stay at an hotel or a home, I chose the latter. I stayed with the editor of 'Y Drych' and his wife. They are very nice people and I enjoyed my stay with them. The editor of one of the local papers came to supper and to interview me. I enclose the result. R. R. Williams is a very nice fellow. You remember him at Newcastle Emlyn – the Grammar

---

[1] Dai Pearce, a loveable, eccentric dairyman who was a deacon at Charing Cross Chapel and who would always pronounce the word as 'pamarama'. The route ML-J is here describing has lost something of its original character on account of the several modern tunnels which keep the road at lower levels.

School – as Williams Penrhyndendeudraeth. Poor fellow, he buried his wife – a girl from Cardigan – three years ago. His two little boys are in school in England.

We had a good day on Sunday. In the Welsh chapel in the morning, I preached on Romans 1:14. the place was full. In the congregation I saw mother. She, and Mrs and Miss Allison were on their way to Niagara Falls. They had been motoring since Thursday morning and had visited several places, such as Washington, Baltimore, etc. Mother spent the day with us, and the others joined after the evening service. The evening service was a joint service of all the churches of the town and was held in the largest chapel. It was packed full. I preached on Aeneas. That was certainly the best service I have had in this country so far. I was given much freedom and power. The ministers were much moved, shaken and impressed. So were the people. Many came to speak to me, and to state their experience and their difficulties. The editor of the paper confessed freely that all his views had been utterly wrong, and asked me, like a little child, to explain the way of salvation to him. He said: 'What I shall put in the paper will be nothing. You cannot be reported.' A crowd of about twelve of us had supper with the Congregational minister afterwards, and we had an excellent chat and discussion. I met four of the best ministers for lunch yesterday, and we discussed theology for about two hours. Then we went to the country, as I have told you. I must confess that I am a bit tired, but it is largely due to lack of sleep. As you know, I am due at Scranton tonight and Philadelphia tomorrow. Then there is nothing until Sunday at New York. Then home! I fear that Mrs Pugh has somehow muddled my letters. I have not received a single letter since a week last Friday – the one you sent the day after I left. I found that it took about two days for letters to get from New York to Columbus. I am looking forward to getting to Scranton, as I feel sure I shall find something from you there. You see, I do not feel for a moment that you have forgotten me! I am sure that Mrs Cynolwyn is somehow responsible. Mother said she had had a letter from Vin[1] on Tuesday morning last

---

[1] His brother, Vincent.

week which had come on the 'Queen Mary'. I wonder how you all are? By a fortnight today D.V. I shall be back with you. I feel about this country exactly as I did about Canada. Well, I must stop. Writing on the train is almost an impossibility.

Look after yourselves now for this next fortnight. I intend to go back to New York on Thursday, and I'll try to write a word then too. I'll not come here without you again. I am more homesick for you than ever. All my love to you, my dear, dear girl,

Ever yours,

Martyn

My very dear remembrances to your Mother and Father, and to the girls and all there. Love M.

A Critical Juncture in 1938[1]

Llanidloes,
10 June, 1938

My Dear Bethan,

Many thanks for phoning last night and for your letter this morning. Elizabeth really has done well, hasn't she? I did not think she had a hope. Mr Hamer says we have every right to postpone the acceptance of this scholarship – that is to ask the authorities to keep it back, until we go to – Bala? – but we shall see. I'm sure Elizabeth must have been very excited when she heard the news. I do not think we need have any worries about her future.

---

[1] This letter from Mid-Wales, typical of the shorter ones which he would send to Bethan if he was away for more than a day preaching elsewhere in Britain, was written during what proved to be the great turning point in his work as a pastor. A fact of great significance was not recorded in his letters to Bethan from the United States in 1937. The ageing Dr Campbell Morgan (minister of Westminster Chapel, London) had heard him preach in Philadelphia and, it appears, determined to seek him as his successor. But in 1938 several other parties were interested in using him, the Free Church Council, Marylebone Presbyterian Church, London (whose call he declined), and the Theological College of his own

Well, I have told you on the phone that all is well with me. I had a very happy time at Gorsedd – quiet, simple people with a very real interest in the Gospel. It is tragic that the preachers are preaching everything except the Gospel, while the people are thirsting for the truth. The sermons I preached to them were Romans 1:14 and John 8:32. I told you this farmer, where I was staying, was farming 850 acres, and milking 150 cows every day. Yesterday morning he took me to have a look at his land and crops and stock, etc.

I had a good journey here yesterday. But it is obvious that I must be tired, for I left my mackintosh in the train, when changing at Welshpool! Very luckily for me, just before my train pulled out, one of the porters came shouting, 'Has any gentleman left an overcoat in the other train?' I realised that I was the man, and I got the coat! I was very glad that I had refused to listen to you, when you were trying to persuade me to take my new coat!

Mr Hamer and I went for a walk last night. The country here is altogether beautiful, and this welcome break, will, I'm sure, do me the world of good. I don't know for certain what are the plans for today.

Don't work too hard, and remember to go to bed early. Half this time is nearly over, and then I shall be back with you. I felt that E. must have a letter this time. All my love to you, the dearest girl in all the world,

Ever yours,

Martyn

---

denomination at Bala in North Wales. As already noted, on 1 May 1938, chiefly on account of his health, ML-J had announced he would terminate his work at Sandfields in July. He was convinced that, whatever happened, he must have a break. Morgan now stepped in, and a strong church meeting at Westminster on May 26 confirmed their minister's proposal that Lloyd-Jones should come to share the ministry for six months. ML-J accepted, thinking, as this letter indicates, that it would provide a breathing space before any permanent appointment – with Bala as his first interest. Instead he was to remain at Westminster Chapel for thirty years.

At the Outbreak of the Second World War[1]

12 Vincent Square,
1 September, 1939

Dear Bethan,

I am writing a short note as promised. The train did not get into Paddington till 7.40 p.m. It was not a bad journey though, on the whole. We had to wait in a queue for a taxi for about half-an-hour, but eventually arrived safely, luggage and all.

By now, of course, you have heard everything on the wireless, and so you know as much as we do. Mother's intention at the moment is to go to Eastcote to sleep,[2] and perhaps to stay. Vincent speaks of going to Hereford for the week-end.[3] I have not had a word with Campbell Morgan nor anyone else yet, of course, so I don't exactly know where I will be tomorrow night. You shall know that, and all my other arrangements, the moment I know.

Vin says that there is a feeling of great confidence here in London, about everything. It is clear Italy is not coming in to the war.

Well, Bethan dear, keep your spirit at peace. Leave yourself and me too, and everything in God's hand and you will find peace and rest. You know what it is to do this in other connections. Do the same now. It was sad to see young wives bidding farewell to their husbands on our way up.

All my love to you dear Bethan and to the children,

Ever yours,

Martyn

[1] After ML-J's acceptance of a temporary position at Westminster Chapel, the family had moved to London in 1938. As from September 1939 he became the permanent colleague of Campbell Morgan although, for the reason stated in the correspondence which follows, it was soon to seem far from permanent. After their summer holidays in 1939 ML-J was with the family in Llanelli, South Wales, for a preaching engagement at the end of August when the imminency of war with Germany became apparent. In that event, an aerial attack on London was anticipated and a sudden evacuation of mothers and children was immediately put into effect. He therefore returned alone to London on 31 August leaving Bethan and the children at Llanelli.

[2] His mother's brother's home near Harrow.

[3] Vincent's family had moved to this town in the West Country.

A Confused Sunday at Westminster Chapel

12 Vincent Square,
Sunday, 3 September, 1939

My Dear Bethan,

I want to catch the 6.00 p.m. so there is no time to say any but the one essential thing, and that is that I have booked a room in the Regent Palace Hotel to sleep every night.[1] I first tried the Dolphin Court but very unfortunately the Government had taken all the rooms. There is not one either in St. Ermins – I tried there yesterday as well as this afternoon. But, as I say, I have been successful in the Regent Palace, and they have complete A.R.P. arrangements there.[2] So now you can be quite happy that I have carried out my promise to you! Mother is going to Eastcote – the family arrived back there this afternoon.

These are strange days. C. M., Marsh[3] and I had agreed yesterday that there should be a service at 6.30 tonight. But, of course, after hearing the news at 10 a.m. we saw that it would be useless to have a service tonight. So there is not to be one, and no one has the slightest idea how the future will plan out. We shall have to wait to see how things go. I was with C. M. in the pulpit this morning – congregation about the same as last Christmas morning.[4] After the reading and the prayer, he had just started reading the report of what Chamberlain had said on the wireless at 11.15 to the people, when the air-raid warning sounded. The service had to be closed at once. The police would allow no one to go out into the street. We hung about in the corridors and the various rooms until the 'all-clear' sounded.

All the people were asking after you, and send their warmest remembrances. I will try to get you on the phone tonight and I

---

[1] This was the day on which war was declared. Bethan, anxious that he should not sleep alone at the old family home at Vincent Square, had received his promise that he would make some other arrangement.

[2] A.R.P. – Air Raid Precautions, particularly a bomb shelter.

[3] Arthur E. Marsh, church secretary at Westminster Chapel for more than fifty years.

[4] Presumably, somewhat less than a usual Sunday.

will write you again tomorrow D.V. I sent the gas masks off yesterday. That's all for now. All my love to you and the girls.

Ever yours,
        Martyn

Notes (1) No gas masks available for children 2–5. I went to the City Hall offices in Charing Cross Road yesterday afternoon. They are being made. When available I will send one on. You can let Theresa[1] have hers. By the way, I think you should give her the week's notice at once. She will understand and will have no difficulty about getting work. (2) Fix E's school if you can at Llanelli. Failing that, Llandilo. It seems clear to me that Westminster will not be able to support C. M. and me.[2] That will mean that I go. In that case, we could not well afford to have her in a residential school. However, if things get better, we might do something later. (3) Vin went to Hereford on the 5.30 p.m. train yesterday. He said he would probably return tomorrow.

        All my love, Martyn.

My warmest regards to all. I have bed and breakfast at the Regent Palace for 10/–. I shall come here [Vincent Square] after breakfast each day, so write here.

Patience amidst Uncertainties

12 Vincent Square,
16 September, 1939

My Dear Bethan,

I was very glad to have your letter this morning and to know that you are all right. As I said in that P.C. last night, I have never had to leave you behind with such a sense of rebellion that I could not do anything to help you.[3] But there it is, nothing could be

---

[1] Their maid from Aberavon who lived with them.

[2] On account of the rapid fall off in congregations that was anticipated in all city churches. His prediction almost came true, see *D. Martyn Lloyd-Jones: The Fight of Faith*, pp. 13–14.

[3] He had been to Llanelli for a brief visit. His diary had long been

done for the moment. I believe that our duty is to try to be patient
for a few weeks until we see how things are to be.[1] As I said in the
P.C., we will be starting on the new order in Westminster: a week
tomorrow morning – at 11.00 and the second service at 2.30 or 3.00.
We shall then see what the effect of this change will be on time and
petrol restrictions too. The likelihood is that by about the end of
October, we shall see clearly what the future is to be. Putting the
Bible School on Saturday afternoon [instead of Friday night] has
been excellent – Miss Howell's idea it seems. C. M. was in a very
good mood last night – his depression had vanished. I think that
the reason for this is that he sees a hope for his future now, with
this new arrangement. It seems that there were about 500 present
last night. Douglas Johnson was there and came back with us to
supper. He was here until about 9.30 p.m. He had nothing new to
say, except to inform me that they had decided that I should remain
'President of the IVF for the duration of the war'![2] Nothing else of
any importance has been happening. Vin is not likely to put his
possessions in store. They charge £4.0.0d. more than the rates. I
have thought and thought again, but I cannot see any better
arrangement than the present one – not for some time, at least. I
have many objections to it, such as (1) too much work for you (2)
lighting fires in the morning (3) cooking and cleaning.[3] But what

---

booked with mid-week preaching engagements for these weeks and
opportunities to be with the family were therefore far less frequent than
they would all have wished.

[1] The uncertainties were many. No one knew whether the absence of
bombing would only to be temporary and whether or not the general
evacuation from the cities would therefore be necessary for a prolonged
period. What congregations and support would remain at Westminster was
also unknown. Black-out regulations would prevent evening services in
the winter (the chapel not being prepared for that eventuality), and ML-J
did not even know whether he, as a medical doctor, might be called up.

[2] Douglas Johnson, General Secretary of the evangelical student movement, the Inter-Varsity Fellowship. ML-J was President until 1943.

[3] Mrs Lloyd-Jones was now looking after herself and the children in
part of the home to which they had come as visitors in August. The above
words – written in an era when residential domestic help was taken for

worries me most is that you will not be eating enough. I do beseech you to be wise in this matter, and to realise that health is more important than other things. There is no need for you to cut back on expense at all. Take care to prepare and eat proper meals. I have no faith in you in this matter – none at all – and it is a very real worry to me. I want you to make a definite promise that you will take care of this, if only because I am making a special request of it.

I have just sent off a parcel to you of Elizabeth's things – bags, galoshes, etc., etc. I'll bring the other things with me when I come down the week after next. Looking forward to that is like looking forward to many months. I have also sent Theresa's parcel including her overcoat. Jack Cooke was in the station with the case – he brought oranges and apples too. Vin is not going to Hereford this week-end. He still cannot decide what to do. Well, that's all for the moment. I do hope you are feeling happier. There were dozens of women and children on the train yesterday – some very little children like Ann. I understand them perfectly, but still feel that they are very unwise.

All my love to you, my dearest girl and to Elizabeth and Ann. I will write again on Monday D.V.

Yours ever,
Martyn

The Difficulty of Being Calvinistic

12 Vincent Square,
22 September, 1939

My Dear Bethan,

Your letters came safely to hand this morning. It is obvious that Elizabeth is beginning to settle down. I wonder if there is any way she can do enough Latin and Geometry to keep up with the form she is in at present? But there, they will have some way of coping

---

granted in many homes – caused her particular amusement when she re-read them in later years.

[45]

with the problem, without a doubt. Nothing of importance to report from here, since I wrote yesterday. I have written the review of D. R. Davies's book, it will probably be in the *Christian World* next week.[1] I was saying to Douglas Johnson, yesterday, that it is very difficult in these present days to be Calvinistic. It is as though one must disagree with everybody – criticising evangelicals and people like D. R. Davies, Brunner, etc., etc. as well. In spite of that, however, it does show that Calvinism is a perfect system, with teaching on every aspect of the truth.

Vin has just gone off to Hereford. He learnt today that he had to be back on Sunday night on account of some appointment on Monday morning. So he decided to go tonight, to have an extra night, or rather not to lose one! The gas, electricity, and telephone are all disconnected in No 24 [Vincent's home] but they'll still have to pay the rates. The difference, in London, between this war and the last is incredible. The best thing ever done, was to pass the Conscription Bill. There are none of the recruiting meetings and the silly excitement of the last, and there are very few soldiers to be seen around.

I think of you preparing breakfast, etc., as I am getting up and doing a few exercises in the mornings. It will be very easy for me to fit in with your arrangements next week when I am with you.

All my love to the dearest girl in the world.

Ever yours,

    Martyn

---

[1] Davies' recently published work, *On to Orthodoxy*, received widespread attention. In a letter to Bethan on 21 September ML-J had said: 'I am in quite a difficulty over the review of D. R. Davies' book. He, like Brunner and Barth falls short of the real thing. I feel he has had some kind of 'intellectual conversion' and nothing more. And yet – on the negative side he is excellent.

Love and 'Instructions'

12 Vincent Square,
25 September, 1939

My Dear Bethan,

Thank you for your letter of this morning, though I am very angry that you should have been up till 11.30 p.m. writing it! I see that you are quite incorrigible![1] The idea that I shall become used to being without you is really funny. I could speak for a long time on the subject. As I have told you many, many times, the passing of the years does nothing but deepen and intensify my love for you. When I think of those days in London in 1925 and '26, when I thought that no greater love was possible, I could laugh. But honestly, during this last year I had come to believe that it was not possible for a man to love his wife more than I loved you. And yet I see that there is no end to love, and that it is still true that 'absence makes the heart grow fonder'. I am quite certain that there is no lover, anywhere, writing to his girl who is quite as mad about her as I am. Indeed I pity those lovers who are not married. Well, I had better put a curb on things or I shall spend the night writing to you without a word of any news.

By the way, the printer's proof of the paper on 'Sanctification' has come, and D. J. wants it back at once, 'with comments'.[2]

We have now found everything on your list and everything is in the little trunk. There is no possibility of bringing the fur coat this time of course, but I'll bring everything else.

As for the 'diet' – it is quite obvious that there is no hope for me to be with you for a meal on Wednesday night, but there will be ample time for me to get something to eat in Cardiff. So don't

---

[1] ML-J did not believe in going early to bed but his wife was still less inclined!

[2] An address he had given the previous summer at the International Conference of Evangelical Students, which became for many years one of the best-selling booklets published by the IVF. Douglas Johnson was universally known by his friends as 'D. J.'

arrange or prepare anything.[1] The uncertainty about the time of the trains confirms the wisdom of this arrangement. With regard to Thursday, I heard from Harris Towy Works this morning, saying that the afternoon meeting is at 2.00 p.m., so I shall have to go there [Carmarthen] in the morning and have dinner with them. The evening meeting is at 5.30. I don't think there is a train back to Llanelli before the 8.30 – arriving Llanelli at 9.00. So the likelihood is that they will make me stay for supper too. So that, as far as Thursday is in question, the only meal that you will have to prepare for me is breakfast. The only 'addition' to my usual is that I now take cornflakes in warm milk after the orange, and then a boiled egg. Remember the wholemeal bread! and the marmite!

I think that completes the instructions! The congregation yesterday morning was down quite a bit as a result of the petrol restrictions. C.M. preached on 'The Eternal God is our refuge, and underneath are the everlasting arms', not really as well as usual. It is sad that his technique prevents him from preaching a message fitting for the times. As for the congregation yesterday afternoon, I don't rightly know what to say. The general feeling was one of pleasurable surprise. I suppose it was more or less like the morning, but very much smaller, of course, than the previous Sunday night. I preached on 1 Samuel 13:19–22. I was given real freedom. Reggie and Rocyn Jones came here to tea. Reggie is sitting his exam this morning. Vin returned last night. Well, I think that is all. As I am preaching morning and afternoon, I am afraid that I shall have no opportunity to write to you. But I will be with you instead of a letter on Wednesday night, I hope – what an ambiguous sentence!

Well, till then, my dear love, and for ever and ever, yours,

    Martyn

All my love to you and the two girls – I have a great longing to see them too.

---

[1] The effect of diet upon health was a life-long interest of ML-J's and his convictions could undergo considerable variations! At this time he was paying particular attention to exercise and diet, and told Bethan proudly in one letter that his weight was now down to eleven stone, one-and-a-half pounds.

Looking for a New Home

12 Vincent Square,
5 November, 1939

My Dear Bethan,

Well, here we are, starting on these three weeks. But for the fact that we can look forward to being with each other continually, I don't know how I could have left you on Friday. But to have this hope to look forward to does change things tremendously, doesn't it?[1] I had quite a good journey – a corner seat all the way from Llanelli. Great crowds came in at every stop. From Swindon on, people were standing all along every corridor. Somewhere between Bridgend and Cardiff, Ellis Edwards' sister – I don't remember her name! – came in to see me. She and some friends were on their way to London. We chatted for a little while.

I tried to get the Haslemere folk[2] on the phone from Paddington, but the answer I got was that all their 'calls' were being transmitted to the house of another doctor. I got the same answer last night. This means that they are away for the weekend, I should think. I wrote them a long and detailed letter last night, and asked them to write to me in North Wales. Yesterday, I called in the offices of the 'Homefinders'. A very nice man dealt with me. According to him, I would not like the bungalows in Brighton, and, as he says, they are twenty minutes from Brighton and that

[1] Their thoughts on the future had clarified to some extent in late October when the deacons at Westminster Chapel had decided that they could continue to support two ministers if the salaries of both were reduced (Campbell Morgan from £1100 p.a. to £800, and ML-J from £700 to £500). He had therefore commenced to look for a home to rent outside the London area but near enough for him to be able to reach Westminster Chapel by train on Sundays.

[2] Dr Gerald Golden and his wife, Dorothy, with whom he had been in touch over possible property in Haslemere, a country town in Surrey, forty-two miles from London.

[49]

makes you wholly dependent on buses.[1]   He showed me a photograph of the flat in Hove that was being advertised for £104 inclusive and it looked very nice. He gave me details of many other places too – one near Caterham which looked quite attractive. He is going to draw up a list for me by next Saturday. It is obvious that there are plenty of places to be had, so you can be quite hopeful. I shall go at it in earnest the minute I get home from the North. Haslemere is the best idea in my opinion, but we'll see.

They had no news to tell here. Vin had gone to Aberayron. He is due back tonight. It seems that Ena [his wife] is coming up this week, and Margaret [maid] is going down to look after the children while he is here! Now *there's* a wife for you worthy of the name, doing, without hesitation, what I wanted you to do! Since Margaret has at last got some job and is due to begin on Saturday, Ena will have to go back before I return from the North.

C. M. and others were asking after you in Westminster yesterday afternoon. Ruth [Morgan] came on the phone at 9 o'clock this morning to know whether I could take the communion service. It seems that C. M. had caught a bit of a cold. Blackie[2] wants him not to preach, but he insists on doing so! I am writing this after breakfast and before going to the Chapel. I will try to send word from somewhere tomorrow. I am due to arrive Holywell about 3.45 p.m. You remember that I am due in Manchester at 12.45 Tuesday. Rhyl address – Harewood, Russell Road.

Well, I think that is all now. I do not know whether you or Ann were the prettier on the station on Friday. All my love to you, the dearest girl in the world, and the two girls,

Ever yours,
    Martyn

[With the help of the Goldens, Haslemere proved to be the location of their next home. They moved to a house there in December where they remained until November 1943.]

---

[1] The family did not own a car until the early 1950s

[2] Margery Blackie, distinguished physician and general practitioner, who was a close friend of the Morgans.

3

TO FRIENDS AND
FELLOW MINISTERS

On his First Sight of the Evangelical Library[1]

12 Vincent Square,
Westminster, S.W.1
4 September, 1939

[To Mr Geoffrey Williams]
Dear Mr Geoffrey Williams,

I write to congratulate you on the wonderful fruits of your labours known as the Beddington Free Grace Library. You will recall that I visited the Library with my friend the Rev. Eliseus Howells the other afternoon.

He and others had already sung its praises, so I came expecting much. Having arrived, and having spent some two and a half hours inspecting the contents, I felt that I was in the precise position of the Queen of Sheba on the occasion of her visit to Solomon.

The collection is remarkable and indeed unique.

As far as I am aware, there is, and can be, no such collection of books anywhere. For anyone who is at all interested in true Protestantism, and especially in its revival in the eighteenth century, the Beddington Free Grace Library is a sheer delight.

[1] This institution, founded by Geoffrey Williams (1886–1975), was to play a major part in ML-J's future life. When it was moved to London, towards the end of the Second World War, he became its President. In an address at the opening ceremony (15 January 1945) ML-J spoke of the desire 'that this Library should become not a museum but a living force' (*Evangelical Quarterly*, April 1945, p. 225). Reporting the occasion, *The Times* (4 February 1945) was correct in anticipating that the work promised 'to be of great significance and far-reaching importance.'

I have but one criticism to offer, and that is with regard to the location of the Library.[1] It should be somewhere in the heart of London within easy reach and access.

As you know, I am prepared to do what I can, not only to make the existence of the Library known, but also to help in more practical ways to bring its treasures within easy reach of all who are interested.

I pray God's continued blessing upon all your self-sacrificing efforts in this great work.

Yours very sincerely,
D. Martyn Lloyd-Jones

Waiting on Divine Guidance

The Haven,
Chatsworth Avenue,
Haslemere, Surrey
19 April, 1940

[To Mr W. Leslie Land][2]
My Dear Land,

Many many thanks for your letter. It is a real privilege to be allowed to share your confidence at such a vital period in your story.

That you are being led clearly and definitely is abundantly

---

[1] At this date it was housed at Mr Williams' house, 'The Brandries', at Beddington in rural Surrey.

[2] W. Leslie Land (1903–86), headmaster of Seaford College Boy's School on the South Coast of England, had invited Lloyd-Jones to preach to his pupils in 1938. A friendship developed and at this point in time Land, convinced that he should turn to the work of the Christian ministry, was looking to ML-J for guidance. In a further letter of 23 May 1940, ML-J, referring to Land's uncertainty said: 'I well know how you feel. I was exactly the same fourteen years ago and, at times, almost despaired. My counsel to you therefore is "let patience have her perfect work".' Land's pastorate at Melbourne Hall, Leicester (1947–61), was to be marked by much fruitfulness. He preached at Westminster Chapel during his friend's summer vacation in the years 1956–58.

evident. The only important thing now is that you are led to the right place and the right sphere for the start. My own experience at the same juncture was that the guidance there again will be equally definite if you will be patient. I thought I was to go to a certain place and I wanted to go there. But it was not to be. When I went to Port Talbot I knew at once it was *the* place. And so it proved to be.

I wish it were possible for us to have a long chat as I am ignorant of many of the facts. To what denomination does your brother's church belong? In the meantime I shall continue to pray for you. Please keep me informed.

My warmest regards,

Yours very sincerely,

D. M. Lloyd-Jones

On Recent News and Books

The Haven,
Chatsworth Avenue,
Haslemere, Surrey,
24 April, 1940

[To Dr Douglas Johnson][1]

My Dear Dr Johnson,

Please forgive me this terrible delay in acknowledging your most kind and interesting letter of last week. Unfortunately I developed one of my attacks of gout on Friday and it made me feel rather rotten during the week-end. Hence the reason also why I did not telephone on Saturday night. I just did nothing except what I was bound to do! I need not say that I am deeply grateful for your kind

---

[1] See above, p. 44. The comparative failure in health, which ML-J experienced in the late 1930s, was at its worst at this point in time and had prevented his attendance at the Inter-Varsity Conference (2–8 April 1940) at Birmingham. Thereafter the problem, which included a measure of depression, largely disappeared, in part, at least, because he learned to know and handle himself better.

interest and suggestion re. the financial position. Actually a kind friend at Westminster has done something in the matter so for the time all is well. And of course my stipend at Westminster is unaffected.

This week, I feel very much better so I hope that from now on I shall continue to make progress. The possibility of seeing you here sometime in May appeals to us all tremendously. That *must* happen, on condition that it will not be too much for you.[1] We must plan more definitely later on.

The account of the Conference was most interesting. Blair seems to have behaved in truly giant fashion. A letter he sent me in reply to mine, expressing my regret at my absence, was in much the same vein. I fear that poor Warner and Aldis could never stand up to him.[2] I gather that the former so praised my book that the book stall was soon sold out!

By the way I had a letter from friend Cutts the other day asking for another book. I told him at the moment my physical condition made it impossible for me to write a best seller.[3] Actually if I did write a book answering Middleton Murry's *The Price of Leadership* I verily believe it would be a best seller. It would also evacuate

---

[1] Johnson himself had been seriously ill earlier in the year.

[2] Duncan McCallum Blair (Regius Professor of Anatomy in Glasgow), and two Anglican ministers, Canon S. M. Warner and the Rev. W. H. Aldis, had been the speakers at the Birmingham conference. The reference to Blair's dominance relates principally to the discussion sessions. 'D. J.' was later to recall that Blair was 'the big leader, the Moses of the 1940 conference, straffing the enemy and unloosing and inspiring our forces'.

[3] Leonard Cutts, publications secretary of the theological section of Hodder and Stoughton, had been responsible for ML-J's first book, *Why Does God Allow War? A General Justification of the Ways of God* (Hodder and Stoughton: London, 1939, and reprinted January 1940). It should be understood that these sentences amount to banter between two friends. ML-J did not take himself seriously as an author, thus, with the exception of his slender work, *The Plight of Man and the Power of God* (Hodder and Stoughton: London, 1942), no further hardback was to appear from him until volume one of *Studies in the Sermon on the Mount* (IVF: London, 1959).

Westminster Chapel of all who claim any relationship to the aristocracy! So it is just as well perhaps that I cannot write it. My thesis would be that the main cause of our present ills is due to the tragic break-down and failure of the middle-class in this country due especially to their aping of the aristocracy especially in sending their children to public schools.[1] However, I must desist.

We shall have to evolve some scheme of life that will suit us both. It will certainly exclude gardening! Many thanks for the —— [indecipherable] book. I have only just dipped into it as yet. Winston Churchill goes from strength to strength. What about Duff Cooper yesterday?[2]

We all join in our warmest regards to you one and all.

Yours very sincerely,

D. M. Lloyd-Jones

The 'Westminster Theological Journal' and other Items

The Haven,
Chatsworth Avenue,
Haslemere, Surrey
8 May, 1940

[To Dr Douglas Johnson]

My Dear Dr Johnson,

I am truly grateful for your letter and the enclosures, especially the *Westminster Theological Journal* which I consider to be first rate. I am so impressed by it that I am determined to see every issue somehow. We must discuss that when we meet. Apart from the articles, the book reviews are excellent. I have not been able to read the Victoria Institute papers as yet. I felt that our friend

---

[1] i.e. fee-paying, private boarding schools in the tradition which held that Wellington had won the battle of Waterloo 'on the playing fields of Eton'.

[2] Prominent member of Parliament who had just returned from a speaking tour in the United States and was soon to become Minister of Information under Churchill (who became Prime Minister in May 1940).

Noddy's article in the *Evangelical Quarterly* was just a little too clever.

W—— [indecipherable] sent me an article written by him several months ago. I have just read it and returned it to him. I do not know what to say of it. It struck me as lacking grip and as being almost boyish. I am sure that *Theology* will not take it. I suggested that he should try the *Evangelical Quarterly*.[1] As far as it goes it is all right but it seems to lack something vital.

I enclose this MS at your request. It is good to know of your continued progress. I am also improving daily – with Miss Hicks[2] still in attendance!

Our united regards to you all as a family,

Yours very sincerely,

D. M. Lloyd-Jones

Living from Day to Day

The Haven,
Chatsworth Avenue,
Haslemere, Surrey
25 November, 1940

[To Mr Leslie Land]

My Dear Land,

The arrival of your letter written on the 21st has almost convinced me of the truth of telepathy! The facts are that I was preaching at Florence Road Baptist Church, Brighton. I travelled there on Wednesday morning and returned again on Thursday evening, passing through Worthing each time. From someone or other I had heard that you were at Worthing. I thought about you on passing through there and my wife and I spoke about you, wondering what was happening to you, etc. Then comes your letter!

---

[1] ML-J and D. J. were becoming increasingly involved in the *Evangelical Quarterly*. The former subsequently became chairman of its board before it passed to new ownership in the 1950s.

[2] A lady who was teaching him better voice production.

Your letter is most interesting. As regards the Church of England I think I mentioned the possibility to you in one of our chats. As far as I am concerned there is nothing whatsoever against it. Indeed, I am not at all sure but that in many ways it would be the right thing for you. I am persuaded that Nonconformity is going to have a real fight for existence after this war. It seems to be the case, in England especially, that the Church has a better opportunity. However you will be led. The matter of a brief training will not worry you. Again I believe there is much to be said in favour of that especially at such a place as the BCMS Bristol. Do please let me know what happens.

As to my affairs, they are certainly in a rather muddled condition. We moved to the Livingstone Hall because a number of people, including Dr Morgan, had become somewhat scared. But it has not been a success and we shall soon be returning to the church. I say 'we' but the whole question of my future is in the melting pot. As we are going on at the moment it is clear that the church cannot continue to support two ministers. We are about £15 to £20 down each Sunday and we are living on a reserve fund collected last year. Dr Morgan has to go on and cannot retire because he is penniless. He has been most improvident and indeed prodigal. At his age and in his infirmity he cannot well go elsewhere. That means that I shall probably go. I offered to do so at the end of September. They would not hear of it then but it seems to me to be quite inevitable.

Then? I do not know. There are certain openings in Wales. But at the moment I am living from day to day. Our congregation at the Livingstone Hall is about 200–215. The second of the two sermons on Luke 12, 4 & 5 gave us great satisfaction. I have preached it several times since.

We all join in warmest regards to Mrs Land and your good self.

Yours very sincerely,

D. M. Lloyd-Jones

More Shared News on Books

The Haven,
Chatsworth Avenue,
Haslemere, Surrey
8 January, 1941

[To Dr Douglas Johnson]
My Dear Dr Johnson,

Herewith the review of John Thomas' book[1] by Van Til. By now you will have returned from the conferences. I hope that both were successful and that you are satisfied with the result.

Were it not that it would mean additional work for you, I should be glad of a report of both and especially what happened to your memorandum.

By the way, I have failed to find those copies of *Theology* with reference to the evangelical vicar of Cheltenham.

I have been reminded by Blackwell's (Oxford) of a book that might interest you. I well remember the excellent reviews of it when it first appeared. It is: *The Political Aspect of Religious Development* by E. E. Thomas. It is listed there at 7/6.

I am at the moment reading a book called *Psychology, Psychotherapy and Evangelicalism* by J. G. McKenzie. I will let you have a full report later. Its effect upon me up to the moment is to make me feel like writing either a very long review or else a book by way of reply! It is very stimulating – in fact too much so after 9.00 p.m.

I hope that you and all the family are well. We are near freezing point here.

With our united warmest regards,
Yours sincerely,
D. M. Lloyd-Jones

---

[1] *Philosophic Foundations* (Westminster City Publishing Co., London). Van Til's review was published in the *Evangelical Quarterly*, 15 April 1941.

The Need for Evangelical Authors

The Haven,
Chatsworth Avenue,
Haslemere, Surrey
3 February, 1942

[To the Rev. Philip E. Hughes][1]
Dear Mr Hughes,

Many many thanks for your extremely kind letter of January 28th.

Believe me, what I said to you was most genuine. I had never heard of your name until I received your paper from Mr Alan Stibbs. At once I was gripped by your style. Then by your subject and finally by your intellectual grasp and power. Above all, of course, the character of your exposition appealed to me tremendously. For years I have bemoaned the fact that as evangelicals we lack scholars and writers. I have been looking out for men constantly. Apart from T. F. Torrance, who is far too Barthian for my liking, you are the only man who has aroused my interest deeply.

I look forward to meeting you sometime in the future, God-willing, and I shall count it a privilege to be of any little help or service to you.

I believe God has great things for you to do.

I find that I have to be in London for a wedding on Saturday February 14th. I might be free by 2.30 p.m. if you could arrange to meet me. We will then have a chat. But if that is not convenient (and please do not cancel any other arrangement for my sake) there

---

[1] The Rev. Philip E. Hughes (1915–90) who had first heard ML-J at the Albert Hall, London, on 3 December 1935, and was, at this time, a curate in a London parish (St John's, Lewisham). This was the start of a life-long friendship. A paper which Hughes had given on original sin had been passed on to ML-J by the Rev. Alan Stibbs (1901–71) of Oak Hill Theological College; it was published in the *Evangelical Quarterly* (James Clarke: London) for July 1942.

is another possibility. A number of us, including Mr Stibbs, have started a new fellowship of evangelical ministers and clergy.[1] I have suggested that all of you who meet with Mr Stibbs be invited.

The next meeting is on March 10th at 10.30 a.m. If you can come to that we could have a long talk afterwards. Please choose the day which suits you best and let me know at your convenience.

With warm regards,

Yours very sincerely,

D. M. Lloyd-Jones

Meeting Douglas Johnson

The Haven,
Chatsworth Avenue,
Haslemere, Surrey
2 March, 1942

[To the Rev. Philip E. Hughes]

Dear Mr Hughes,

Many thanks for your kind letter.

I am glad Dr Johnson is seeing you tomorrow. Be quite free with him. I am sure that he will be able to arrange things for you. He is an excellent man, in many ways the most important person in evangelical circles in these days.

I shall hear the result of your meeting later.

I shall be glad to have lunch with you after the meeting on the 10th. I have an appointment during the afternoon, but the lunch interval will give us time for a good chat. I enclose the Dr Williams' Library form.

In great haste and with warmest regards and greetings,

Yours very sincerely,

D. M. Lloyd-Jones

[1] A fraternal of ministers under his chairmanship at Westminster Chapel which became known as the Westminster Fellowship.

A Word for a Young Minister

The Haven,
Chatsworth Avenue,
Haslemere, Surrey
3 March, 1942

[To the Rev. Kenneth J. MacLeay]
Dear Mr MacLeay,[1]

Many many thanks for your extremely kind and valuable letter of February 23rd. I am truly sorry to find that you were at Westminster Chapel without coming to see me. If ever you come again please do not fail to come to speak to me.

I am most interested and encouraged to hear what you have to say about the friends who came with you to the service. Please tell them that I shall be glad to meet them at any time, and if I can be of any service to them I shall esteem it a privilege.

And now let me thank you for your kind gift to our church funds. You really should not have done this as it is not intended for ministers like yourself. However I am truly grateful to you. You will get the official receipt from the Church Secretary. He is also arranging to let you have the *Westminster Record* regularly and will forward also the back numbers for this year. I hope you will find it of some value were it only as a general stimulant.

I trust that you will be much blessed in your charge and in the work. The times are difficult and we must be patient. The only hope, I see more and more clearly, is a Revival. I feel we are all

---

[1] Kenneth J. MacLeay (1905–83), minister of the Free Church of Scotland, was born in Sleat, Skye, and a seaman before his conversion. Thereafter he studied for the ministry (1937–41), and was ordained to the charge of Lochinver in his native Scottish Highlands in 1942. The following year he married his life-long helper, Jessie Coull. In 1946 he was called to Beauly, Easter Ross, where he remained until retirement in 1978. Like Dr Lloyd-Jones, Mr MacLeay loved good books, old-school, experimental Christianity and he was a great helper of younger men. See *Diary of Kenneth MacRae,* ed. Iain H. Murray (Edinburgh: Banner of Truth, 1980).

called to pray and to prepare for such a movement. Nothing else can possibly deal with the terrible state of the country and of the world. In any case our business is to sow the seed in hope, knowing that God alone can give the increase. Do not allow the devil therefore to discourage you.

I find nothing so refreshing to my soul as to read the accounts of revivals in the past. It is good also to read sermons and other works by servants whom God has honoured such as Spurgeon, Moody, Finney[1] etc.

If I can be of any help in any way please do not hesitate to write to me. May the Lord bless you abundantly in all things and use you to His glory,

Yours very sincerely,

D. M. Lloyd-Jones

Hughes' Arrival in South Africa and News of Westminster

The Haven,
Chatsworth Avenue,
Haslemere, Surrey
15 June, 1942

[To the Rev. Philip E. Hughes]
My Dear Friend,

I return herewith the MS of your article on 'the Virgin Birth'. I have read it with the greatest possible interest and pleasure and indeed edification. I believe it to be better than the one on 'Original Guilt'. As regards the literary character that is most definitely the case. The style is excellent and your quotations are well chosen and most aptly employed. The article is indeed a fine blend of literary grace and scholarship – the two essential qualities

---

[1] In ML-J's later judgment Finney was a 'Pelagian': 'Scripture was twisted and forced to fit into his rationalistic scheme'. *The Puritans: Their Origins and Successors* (Edinburgh: Banner of Truth, 1987), pp. 314–16.

in a writer. I say nothing of course about the orthodoxy of your position or the spirit of deep devotion that informs the entire article. It must be printed. I suggest you send it to Professor Maclean whose address is: 53 Leamington Terrace, Edinburgh 10. Tell him that I have suggested your doing so.[1]

Have I any criticisms or suggestions to make? There is really but one which is of any importance. You must do something about the first paragraph. Had I not known you I would have taken all that as representing *your* views, and perhaps I would have read no further. You must indicate somehow that you are but stating the case of the enemy. There are several ways you can do that. You can put the whole paragraph in the form of a quotation and then add the words – 'so the modern pundits' or something like that. You will know how to do that best but it must be done. I am not sure but that quotation marks alone will be enough.

I am glad that a mere speaker like myself should have caught you out in places that I have ventured to underline in pencil and where I charge you with coining words! See 'indefaceably' on page 9 instead of 'ineffaceably', 'indefection' on page 9 and 'Preservator' also on page 9. 'Indispensible' on page 8 is a mere typing error obviously.

I have been consulting my diary as to our next meeting. I fear that I see no hope before Wednesday July 15th. I wonder whether you could meet me for tea that day at the National Club? Let me know later at your convenience. I am sorry that really urgent business matters which I had to transact with Douglas Johnson last Tuesday prevented my seeing you properly. I was glad to see that you looked well.

My kindest regards,
Yours very sincerely,
    D. M. Lloyd-Jones

---

[1] It was published in the *Evangelical Quarterly* under the title, 'The Son of the Highest', October 1942.

Thoughts on Authors

The Haven,
Chatsworth Avenue,
Haslemere, Surrey
17 April, 1943

[To Mr Leslie Land]
My Dear Land,

Your letter of this morning came as a very pleasant surprise. Many many times have I thought of you and wondered how you were. Especially when we heard report of air-raids on Worthing. Indeed various things have made us speak of you from time to time. But now comes your letter with the good news not only that you are safe and sound but also exceptionally well. I must hear all about 'The Reformed Diet' (what a good name!) sometime. It sounds good.

I am glad to say that we are all well and that we have had a good winter. I have done a great deal of travelling recently and find that I have been able to stand up to it much better than I could have done at any time during the past four years. You will be glad to hear also that our congregations at Westminster have been slowly but definitely increasing in size. And in addition to that many have remarked on the intense listening. The main task there is to turn an intellectual listening into a vital one. You will know what I mean by that.

I agree entirely with what you say about Niebuhr.[1] Like so many of these men he has undergone a philosophical conversion. They are all right until they come to the Bible. Philosophically speaking I still find that Niebuhr's book is one of the best for many years.

---

[1] Karl Paul Reinhold Niebuhr (1892–1971), American theologian, of German parentage, and of neo-orthodox and liberal views. The book referred to by Land was Niebuhr's *The Nature and Destiny of Man,* vol. 1, 1941. The second volume was to be published after this letter was written in 1943.

We shall be able to see more exactly where he is when vol. 2 appears. But I am not too hopeful.

If you have Micklem's[1] Lent book in mind, I was frankly disappointed with it. He allows his doctrine to be determined by his sentiment and seems to me constantly to give the whole case away. He is the victim of his own geniality. I fear he is an essayist rather than a theologian. By the way have you read the book *Christus Victor* by Aulén to which he refers? It is excellent. I read it when it first appeared several years ago. Publishers SPCK. I have read nothing big during the past winter largely because nothing really big has appeared. As lighter reading I have read *Retrospect on an Unimportant Life* by Hensley Henson.[2] It is a sheer delight from the standpoint of style. Important also as a history of the C. of E. during the past fifty and sixty years. Illuminating also as an illustration of the difference between a humanist and a Christian.

More and more am I being drawn to see that the greatest need today is the power of the Holy Spirit in and through individuals. Right theology is essential but without the power given by the Spirit it can achieve nothing. So many say that theology therefore matters nothing. I reply – 'You cannot have a true and valuable fire without first setting the paper and the wood and the coal. A fire made of shavings soon gives out.'

My wife joins me in sending love to Mrs Land and your good self. Also Peter. Do come and see us soon.

Yours very sincerely,

D. M. Lloyd-Jones

---

[1] Nathaniel Micklem (1888–1976), Congregational and ecumenical leader. At first friendly to ML-J, he made him the subject of a critical, anonymous review in the *British Weekly* in March 1953. See *D. Martyn Lloyd-Jones: The Fight of Faith,* pp. 16, 228, 230.

[2] Anglican Bishop of Durham.

Opinions on MSS and News

39 Mount Park Crescent,
Ealing, London W.5
17 April, 1946

[To the Rev. Philip E. Hughes]
My Dear Philip,

Your letter which arrived on Monday has once more filled me with a sense of shame at my great failure as a correspondent.

I need not weary you by detailing again the cause and explanation. I can honestly say this. My failure to write is not due to forgetfulness of you. Not a day passes but that I think of you and pray for you. My correspondence and work have reached such proportions that I have had to have the help of a lady shorthand typist. Several times I have been on the verge of dictating a letter to you, but always I have felt that that somehow would not do. I had intended writing to you this week in any case. Your letter but served to 'heap coals of fire on my head'! I know that you forgive me.

I do not think I have ever thanked your good and kind wife for the excellent jar of marmalade which she sent us and which was greatly enjoyed. I do so now most sincerely.

I scarcely know where to begin.

First let me start with what you say in your letter about thoughts of visiting England next year. Nothing could give us greater joy and I do hope you will find it possible to arrange it. One word of warning! It is more than likely that I shall, D.V., be in the States and Canada during the period mid-July to mid-September 1947. Therefore avoid that time in your proposed visit at all costs.

I am particularly interested in what you record of your present thoughts concerning yourself, your work and your future. It is precisely what I have always felt about you. That was why I was so grieved about your return to Africa. But I admired the way in which you felt that you must honour your pledge and vow. But I have no doubt at all that you are meant to use that outstanding gift that God has given you in the matter of writing and I am sure that in good time He will show you what you are to do. I am particularly glad that you are doing the B.D. and that you propose to do the M.Th. also. They will all be very useful for the future.

Your two articles arrived safely. 'Time, Progress and Eternity' I think is excellent and shows you at your best. I found the opening philosophical part at the beginning a bit beyond me, as I always tend to do with pure philosophy. But as for the rest I thought it first-rate. I don't know what the *Evangelical Quarterly* people will do about it. They are having much material these days. Hence many articles are much delayed. I do not think that they shall regard it as being too philosophical. I shall let you know when I hear from them. Or they may write directly to you.

About the booklet on The Cross for the IVF. I am not quite as happy. You say that you yourself were not too pleased with it and that you wrote it in a hurry. I shall say that it is the poorest thing that I have read by you. I have discussed it with Mr Inchley[1] and he will indicate matters of detail to you. I feel you allowed yourself to be over-influenced by the fact that it was to be for school-boys. You seem to be writing down to their level and striving to be 'devotional' in style. It is unlike you and I feel unworthy of you. Furthermore I feel that it has made the subjective aspect too prominent, almost to the extent of teaching the 'moral influence' theory.[2] I know that you do not believe that. My feeling is, as I say, that you felt that a certain form was prescribed and that influenced your thought. I would say quite definitely that you should not in future attempt anything along that line. You must write for men and leave the other to those who cannot write for men!

The one or two line expressions which Mr Inchley indicates to you are, I feel, to be explained in the same way. I hope you will not think that I have been unduly critical and I know that much can be said on the other side. But I always feel that nothing is more important than that the objectivity of the atonement should be kept absolutely clear and that our reactions and sensations should

---

[1] Ronald Inchley, Publications Manager of IVF.

[2] i.e., that the cross influences people by being a demonstration of God's love and character.

never be allowed to become a part of our understanding of what happened there or in any way influence the efficacy of what happened.[1]

I shall be most interested to hear your comment. Were I not jealous for your reputation, and so concerned that nothing under your name should be published except that which is first-class, I should never have raised these points. As for the IVF people they would almost certainly have printed your MS practically as it is!

Keep up your writing and send along anything you would like me to read and forward to the *Evangelical Quarterly*. I should have said that as regards style and literary flair and ability both articles are what we would expect from you. Your gift of language and expression is truly remarkable.

You will be glad to know that the work at Westminster is progressing favourably. Our congregations have been steadily increasing since the end of the war and we are having congregations both morning and evening of about 850 to 900 people. We are also seeing occasional conversions. But the general state of the people in London and in the country is one of apathy and deadness. Mr Tom B. Rees created a bit of excitement with a campaign at the Westminster Central Hall for six Saturday nights in the winter. But he drew Christians almost entirely and much time was spent in singing choruses.[2] There is a levity and carnality about such efforts which I simply cannot reconcile with the New Testament. There is no hope apart from revival. The Church of England report *Towards the Conversion of England* you have probably seen.[3] It is the old story and they still believe that they can organise these things. Nothing but an unusual and signal manifestation of

---

[1] A real transfer of guilt took place at Calvary. The redemption there accomplished is applied by God to the church and does not *depend* upon man's response.

[2] Tom Rees (1911–70), evangelist and founder of Hildenborough Hall, Kent, in 1945. It may well be that he primarily drew young people of church background but that many of them were unconverted when they first heard him this writer and his wife can personally confirm.

[3] The report, prepared by a committee under the chairmanship of Dr Chavasse, Bishop of Rochester, was published in 1945.

God's power through the Holy Spirit can possibly meet the present need. I pray daily for revival and try to exhort my people to do the same. I am particularly glad that you are being led in the same direction and that you are reading along these lines.

'Reading' brings me to what I fear must be my last topic this time. I am truly grateful to you for these catalogues which you kindly sent me from the USA. I got Douglas Johnson to order Pink's book on the Sovereignty of God and Mauro's book on Daniel but I have not had time to read them as yet.

I wonder whether you have seen *Prophecy and the Church* by Oswald T. Allis. It is published by the Presbyterian and Reformed Publishing Company of Philadelphia. It is a devastating attack on Dispensationalism in general and the Scofield Bible in particular. But it is also instructive. It is one of the best books I have ever read on the subject of prophecy if not indeed the best. A smaller book on the same subject by W. J. Grier is published by the Evangelical Book-store, Belfast at 3/- and is also excellent. We have sold large numbers of them at our book-room in Westminster.

At the moment I am just finishing a book by Dr Cornelius Van Til called *The New Modernism*. It is published by the Presbyterian and Reformed Publishing Co of Philadelphia at $3.75. It is an onslaught on Barthianism. The very title will indicate his attitude to you. It is a highly technical and philosophical work. You must read it. It is certainly the most serious attack that has yet been made on Barth whom Van Til accuses of being more opposed to Protestant orthodoxy than he is to modernism. I await with much interest the reviews and comments of the various Barthians in this country.

Another book which has just arrived from the USA is *The Infallible Word* – a symposium by the members of the Faculty of the Westminster Seminary, Philadelphia and published by the Presbyterian Guardian Publishing Corporation, 1505 Race Street, Philadelphia 2, priced at $2.50. It looks really good and is much needed at the present time with all the arguments on the question of authority.

These seem to me the more important books to which I should draw your attention. You may of course have heard of them already. Please let me have your comment if and when you have read them.

All these things are of real importance but more and more I feel that my present need is 'to know Him and the power of His resurrection and the fellowship of His sufferings'. Clear ideas are vital and clear thinking but that is not enough. I feel my love to Him is so cold and so poor and so weak. Yet He is gracious and kind.

We all join in warmest greetings to your good lady and yourself.

Yours very sincerely,

D. M. Lloyd-Jones

P.S. Elizabeth having passed her Higher Certificate with distinction in English is now waiting to enter London University.

Arrangements to Meet

39 Mount Park Crescent,
Ealing, London W.5
8 July, 1947

[To the Rev. Philip E. Hughes][1]

My Dear Philip,

Many thanks for your letter. Glad to know that you are coming up on Friday.

This is my position. I am pledged already to:

(1) Meet and have tea at the National Club with a student from Spurgeon's College at 5.00 p.m.

(2) Interview a woman at Westminster Chapel at 6.00 p.m.

(3) Meeting at Westminster at 6.30 p.m. Dinner after the meeting is not possible for two reasons: 1. They dine at 7.00 p.m. and I am never away from the meeting until about 8.10 p.m. 2. I am generally very tired after the meeting.

I wonder whether you could be at the Club by 4.00 p.m.? We

---

[1] Hughes had returned from South Africa after the war. This brief letter is included because it is typical of many such which ML-J wrote and it also gives some idea of his usual Friday schedule.

could then talk for an hour before my appointment at 5.00 p.m. and we might be able to fix something for Saturday or Sunday. I fear that by next weekend we shall be more or less in a state of chaos here as we are not only going away on the 16th but also hoping to leave this house in a reasonable state for our friends who are going to occupy it while we shall be away.

Kindly let me know whether I come to meet you at The National Club on Friday at 4.00 p.m. either by P.C. or else by telephone after you arrive on Friday (telephone – Perivale 2911).

We all join in sending our love to you both,

Yours very sincerely,

D. M. Lloyd-Jones

Concern Over Hughes' Health and Future Work

39 Mount Park Crescent,
Ealing, London W.5
11 March, 1949

[To the Rev. Philip E. Hughes]

My Dear Philip,

Your letter and the enclosures reached me safely. I cannot tell you how distressed I was by the content of your letter. You must never feel that you are worrying me. I assure you that it is always a joy to hear from you and to see you. I believe that I am serving God by doing everything that I can to help or encourage you. As I have told you before, and as I constantly tell other people about you, you are the only man I have discerned in the past twenty years amongst the younger men who has a theological mind and a real ability in the matter of writing. That has been my main concern always with respect to you, even more important than the personal love and esteem which have grown steadily ever since we first met.

Thus, for every reason, I am concerned as to Dr Todd's report.[1]

---

[1] A. B. Todd was a highly-regarded consultant who ran a nursing home near Bristol. ML-J was himself to undergo treatment there later this same year (*D. Martyn Lloyd-Jones: The Fight of Faith*, p. 208). Philip Hughes

However, knowing Dr Todd as I do, I am not unduly alarmed. He is a genius but has many of the faults of geniuses, especially a tendency to be controlled by his own theories. He is also a natural pessimist. You can never be worse than Todd says! My conclusion is therefore that you have been overworking seriously since you have been at Bristol but there is no real cause for alarm. You must certainly do less but I am not convinced that it is essential for you to return to South Africa.

I am not in a position to say anything definite at the moment, but I beg of you not to take any decision or any irrevocable step for the time being, certainly not until your period at Newton Abbot has ended. I have already made certain moves but I cannot anticipate exactly what they will lead to for a few weeks. I will write to you the moment I have anything definite to say.

In the meantime, therefore, relax and enjoy the rest and change as much as you can. I am more than ever convinced that God has a great work for you to do and that in a theological sense.

As to the paper on 'Infallibility' I think it is excellent. If I have any criticism to offer it is that it does not come sufficiently to grips with the Barthians. I imagine also that many of the men who were present at Rose Hill, Reading, at our conference would also say that it does not deal with the detailed difficulties sufficiently. In other words, it is a bit too general and philosophical!

I am not really happy also about the use of the *testimonium Spiritus internum* as an argument in connection with infallibility. As an argument in connection with its being the Word of God, yes, but in connection with infallibility it seems to me to come perilously near the Barthian position of saying 'it is infallible to me' but not to others. I should have thought that in connection with infallibility, *externum* is more important than the *internum*. However!

By the way I listened to Emil Brunner give a lecture at Kings

---

had been teaching at the BCMS College at Bristol and his present illness, and perhaps other factors, had led him to doubt his continuance in that work. He appears also to have been helping in an Anglican parish.

College on Tuesday evening on 'Predestination and Human Free-dom'. He was very stimulating. He came to listen to me on Sunday evening and came to see me at the close of the service!

I have a very heavy week in North Wales next week. Please remember me.

We all join in much love to you both, and I assure you that it is my daily joy and privilege to remember you in my prayers,

Yours ever sincerely,

D. M. Lloyd-Jones

The First Puritan Conference

39 Mount Park Crescent,
Ealing, London W.5
2 December, 1950

[To the Rev. Philip E. Hughes]

My Dear Philip,

Many thanks for your very kind letter. I would like to say that I greatly enjoyed being with you. It is a pity that we do not have more frequent opportunities of talking together about the things that really matter.

I send this hurried note to let you know that the Conference on the Puritans[1] is due at Westminster Chapel on Tuesday, 19th December, and Wednesday, 20th December. There are three sessions each day, morning, afternoon and evening. I do hope that you will be able to be with us. The Secretary is

Mr James Packer, B.A., Wycliffe Hall, Oxford.

We all join in warmest regards to you both.

Yours very sincerely,

D. M. Lloyd-Jones

---

[1] For the origins of what was soon to become an influential confer-ence see *D. Martyn Lloyd-Jones: The Fight of Faith*, pp. 226–7.

On Breakdowns in the Ministry

39 Mount Park Crescent,
Ealing, London W.5.
March 26, 1957

[To the Rev. Leslie Land]
My Dear Land,

I cannot tell you how sorry I was to hear from one of your members who happened to be visiting London that you were not well.

I gather that it is entirely due to over-work, and, knowing you, I am not at all surprised.

It has been a great source of grief to me that our busy lives have prevented our seeing one another as frequently as I should like. But I often think of you and pray for you and I have been over-joyed to hear of the great and manifest blessing that has attended your ministry at Leicester.

Your present trouble is only temporary. It is quite a common happening at your age and it will in no way affect you permanently. In my medical days I saw many ministers like that and I have seen still more since I have been in the ministry myself.

I have also frequently observed in reading ministerial biographies how often it happens in the forties. It happened to Charles Simeon amongst others.

And, coming down the scale (!) even the redoubtable and insensitive Sidlow Baxter had to take six months off a few years ago. Indeed I myself, as you may remember, had a very bad patch around 1940. Had I not left my church in South Wales when I did and come to Westminster where I had but to preach once a Sunday I am sure I would have gone down.

So you see that it is quite a common experience and one from which the patient invariably makes a complete recovery.

But I must give you some advice which will hasten your recovery. Let me tabulate it.

(1) Do not analyse your symptoms. Still less be worried about

them. Our nervous system can play all sorts of tricks with us and if we begin to consider each symptom we can become very worried. Avoid that.

Just relax completely and give nature a chance.

(2) Don't be in too much of a hurry. Reconcile yourself to the fact that for the time being you must just do nothing. That is the way to prepare for the future.

(3) Do not think at all about the work at Leicester. It is God's, not yours and He will care for it.

(4) You will find that this experience will be most rewarding spiritually. It will bring you as it has brought me to rest more in the love and perfect wisdom of God. I am sure that He has something special for you in all this for which you will thank Him all your life. It will enrich your ministry.

Rest in Him and abandon yourself entirely to Him.

I know that you are doing all this already, but I also know that the devil always takes advantage of fatigue or any physical disability and always tries to discourage! His one object only and always is to separate us from Christ, if he can do that by making us concentrate on ourselves, our symptoms, our work, or our future, he is content.

He can only be met and conquered in the Name of Christ. Do not listen to him therefore. Tell him that you are in the hands of Christ and that you are leaving all things to Him.

Your people at Leicester who love you so dearly and value your ministry so highly are praying for you and your many friends elsewhere, among whom I am happy to count myself, are doing likewise.

My wife and the girls join me in warmest regards,
Yours ever sincerely,
    D. M. Lloyd-Jones

The Possibility of a Bedfordshire Living

39 Mount Park Crescent,
Ealing, London W.5.
23 September, 1964

[To the Rev. J. Gwyn-Thomas][1]
My dear Friend,

You will be surprised to hear from me. Here is the reason.

A great friend of ours – Dr Margery Blackie put to us last night this question: 'Do you know an evangelical vicar who would like a parish with a real opportunity?' These are the facts. Mrs Shuttleworth of Old Wardens Park, Biggleswade, has the gift of the living in her village which is just outside Biggleswade. The village itself consists of some 300 people *but* there is an agricultural college there of some 150 students to which the vicar has access and the students attend the church.

Mrs Shuttleworth is a patient of Dr Blackie's and also a friend. While the latter attends Westminster Chapel regularly, I do not know if the former is evangelical or not. But she is most anxious to get a good man and, as I say, asked Dr Blackie for help for that reason. Biggleswade is in Bedfordshire, 45 miles from London, $11\frac{3}{4}$ from Bedford, 22 miles from Cambridge, etc.

I mentioned you at once and Dr Blackie, having spoken to Mrs Shuttleworth this morning on the telephone, phoned to ask me to write to you at once.

If you are at all interested please write direct to Mrs Shuttleworth stating you are the friend of whom I spoke to Dr Blackie. You will know what to do from there on.

---

[1] The Rev. John Gwyn-Thomas (1923–77), rector of Illogan with Portreath and Trevenson, Cornwall, and a friend with whom ML-J maintained regular contact. The Cornish ministry had been a difficult one. Nothing came of this letter but in 1965 Mr Gwyn-Thomas became vicar of St Paul's, Cambridge.

Well, I have done my duty and can now but pray that you may be given clear guidance. I hope you are all well. Christopher no doubt is back at school again.

Yours very sincerely,

D. M. Lloyd-Jones

4

WESTMINSTER CHAPEL

Consolation for a War-Widow

The Haven,
Chatsworth Avenue,
Haslemere, Surrey
22 January, 1942

[To Dr Anne Connan]¹
Dear Dr Connan,

I cannot tell you how shocked I was to hear the news of the passing of your dear husband from Commander Hollingworth this morning on the phone.

And yet, at a time like this, it is something which happens constantly. At once I thought of your last letter to me in which you stated that you had a sense of foreboding.

---

¹ Carl Johan Bruhn, a Dane studying medicine in Britain, and his wife, Anne (née Connan), began attending Westminster soon after ML-J's arrival and were both greatly helped by his ministry. ML-J's counsel influenced Bruhn against going to war-torn Finland, to aid the Red Cross, before he had qualified. But with his native land overrun by the German army there was no detaining him in Britain. He died on the night of December 28–29 when his parachute failed to open as he was dropped to join the forces of the Danish Resistance. Anne Connan, also qualified in medicine, frequently used her maiden name. For most of her life she remained at Westminster Chapel, and wrote to me of ML-J's ministry: 'He so exalted the Lord Christ, and never obtruded himself, that he created a real thirst in me for the Living God, but never left me with a feeling of self-satisfaction, neither so deflated as to be near despair' (letter of 15 December 1973). There is no record of how many others, similarly connected to Westminster Chapel, were lost in the Second World War.

It is very difficult in a few words to say what I would like to say to you. And as we shall probably arrange a Memorial service it is perhaps unnecessary. I write therefore simply to assure you of the deepest sympathy of my wife and myself. We feel for you more than we can tell you. But it is good to know that you will not mourn 'as those without hope'. It is at such a time as this that one realises the full value of the Christian faith. Were this life and this world all, how terrible would be the outlook. More than that 'God giveth more grace' and you will not be left to yourself.

As for your dear husband he impressed me always, as he must have impressed all who met him, as being a sterling character and a noble man. I cannot but feel that everything seemed to point to a completion in his life. After all the struggle and obstacles he qualified. And then he was able to go on to give the service which he had been longing to give for so long.

I have not heard the details of what happened, but I am certain that calmly and deliberately he sacrificed his life for freedom, truth and honour against the hateful tyranny of Nazism. I shall always be glad to have known him. I recall how he asked me one of the last times, if not the last time I saw him, for the exact reference of words I had quoted in my sermon from the end of Romans 8. Those words I could see meant much to him.

In his letter-card to me informing me of his having to go on active service his one concern was about you. That was why he asked me to write to you.

That you will prove more than worthy of all that he thought of you and expected for you I have no doubt at all.

Probably you feel that all you had planned and looked forward to has suddenly gone, but however hard it is, you will believe won't you that God knows best and 'all things work together for good to them that love God.'

May the God of all consolation comfort and sustain and strengthen you.

With deepest sympathy,

Yours very sincerely,

D. M. Lloyd-Jones

Sympathy and Notes of a Sermon

The Haven,
Chatsworth Avenue,
Haslemere, Surrey
22 January, 1942

[To Mr A. G. Secrett][1]

My Dear Mr Secrett,

Many thanks for your kind letter of this morning and the enclosures.

I was truly sorry to hear last Sunday that you were not well again. And I regret to find from this morning's letter that you are still not right. We must have a long chat together about all this and as to what you should do.[2] This very cold weather may well have something to do with it. So keep warm until you are quite well again.

Your forecast for my text for next Sunday afternoon is quite correct! Actually when I began I had not intended travelling along this line but more and more I felt driven to it.

As you are not likely to be there you may be interested to know that my three main points are to be:

1. Doctrine leads to action and action is always based upon belief.

2. Action cannot be *sustained* in the absence of doctrine.

3. There is only one doctrine that can sustain action – that unfolded by Paul about the resurrection. This does so:

(a) By assuring me of my reward.

(b) By showing me that what I do is part of His great plan which will certainly be fulfilled.

Therefore I must abound in the work of the Lord always. The

---

[1] A. G. Secrett (d. 1973), one of his most trusted deacons.

[2] ML-J was, as this sentence indicates, very ready to give medical advice to friends.

more the better for both the above reasons. I fear I shall have a lot to say to our friend Milligan as I develop the theme.

Our united warmest regards to Mrs Secrett and yourself,

D. M. Lloyd-Jones

Thankfulness for his Support

The Haven,
Chatsworth Avenue,
Haslemere, Surrey
10 April, 1943

[To Mr A. G. Secrett]

Dear Mr Secrett,

It is more than likely that I shall see you tomorrow. Nevertheless I write to you now because I feel that what I desire to say cannot be expressed properly in words face to face. It is one of those rare occasions when the written word improves the spoken.

I write to thank you for what is only adequately described as your brotherly love in presenting me with this excellent suit-case. I chose the word because kindness is not enough. It is more than that and is born of true Christian love.

As for the bag itself it is really excellent and precisely what I desired. It is longer than the one which was stolen but in weight it is actually less. It therefore fulfills both the requirements which I had specially in mind. As I go on my travels it will be a perpetual reminder to me of you and of all you mean to me.

I have told you before of what you have meant to me as regards my ministry at Westminster. You can never know what it means to have someone who is in such sympathy with the message and from every standpoint. Coming as I did from a warm-hearted community where I was surrounded by men and women whose main and supreme interest in life was the Gospel and who delighted in discussing it, and the problems which it raises, more than anything else, I felt terribly lonely at Westminster for the whole of the first year. Indeed I could scarcely believe that it was actually possible for a church to be so spiritually cold.

The night we met Mrs Secrett and yourself at the Davies' was a most significant event. I saw at once a complete unity and affinity of spirit. And it has continued ever since. I need not say that I thank God for you and for all you mean. As for all your kindness in the housing matter during the past weeks words fail me.[1] Your judgement is our sheet-anchor.

As I shall tell you tomorrow, my wife's scruples have decided that we shall not view the house tomorrow but wait another opportunity. I think she is right – 'whatsoever is not of faith is sin'. 'All things are lawful but all things are not expedient.'

We all join in much love to Mrs Secrett and your good self.

Yours very sincerely,

D. M. Lloyd-Jones

Increase at the Chapel

The Haven,
Chatsworth Avenue,
Haslemere, Surrey
21 May, 1943

[To Mr Hector Brooke][2]

Dear Mr Brooke,

I feel I must write to thank you for your kind and encouraging letter. In days like these a word like this is truly 'a cup of cold water'.

---

[1] Mr Secrett, a builder in Ealing, had been helping them to look for a home in London. They moved from Haslemere to 2 Colebrooke Avenue, Ealing, in November 1943. See p. 99 below.

[2] Hector Ryland Brooke (1900–77), for many years a prayerful supporter of the ministry of ML-J and of the movement which saw a recovery of the doctrines of grace in England. From his home at Malvern, and subsequently at Bath, he followed everything which affected the cause of the gospel with the deepest interest. A fine description of one service at Westminster Chapel in 1948, which Brooke attended with his wife, Greeba, will be found in *D. Martyn Lloyd-Jones: The Fight of Faith*, p. 191.

The heavy air-raids in 1940–41 scattered our congregation which until then had been very well maintained. Actually we are slowly improving and increasing at the present time. Last Sunday night's congregation was one of the best we have had for nearly three years!

I shall greatly value your prayers. The supreme need of the hour is intense prayer for spiritual revival on the part of Christian people.

Again my warmest thanks and with all good wishes,

Yours sincerely,

D. M. Lloyd-Jones

P.S. When you are next at Westminster please come in to see me if you can spare the time.

Annual Letter, 1947[1]

Westminster Chapel,
Buckingham Gate,
London S.W.1
1 January, 1947

[To the Members of Westminster Chapel]

Dear Friend,

It is my privilege once more at the beginning of a New Year to send you a word of greeting in the name of Christ.

The feeling that is uppermost in my heart as I do so is one of deep gratitude to God for all His goodness to us during another year.

It is agreed generally that this past year has been one of great, and in many ways unexpected, difficulties in most realms. The cessation of hostilities has not brought the release and the relief that had been anticipated, nor a relaxation of the sense of strain and tension. The return to conditions of peace has been delayed. All

---

[1] Somewhat earlier ML-J had begun to write an annual letter for every member at Westminster though this is the first we have been able to find. Other such annual letters followed until the end of his ministry at the Chapel.

this has its inevitable effect upon the life of a church, and particularly a church like ours.

It is in the light of such a situation that we thank God for His goodness to us, and for the measure of encouragement He has been pleased to grant us. The steady increase in the size of the congregations both morning and evening has been noticeable. We have had the pleasure of receiving a large number of friends into the full membership of the church. But above all else we rejoice in the fact that God has been pleased to bless the preaching of the word to the conversion of many souls. It has ever been my view, on my understanding of the New Testament, that the work of evangelism is to be done regularly by the local church and not by sporadic efforts and campaigns. More and more as modern influences tend to disintegrate and disrupt the recognised and divinely ordered units in life, such as the family and the home, shall we need to stress the unique value and importance of the church and church life as the vital unit in the spiritual realm. The glory of life in the church is that it is corporate without violating individual personality as is done by crowds and mass meetings and movements.

As we face the future we are more determined than ever 'not to know any thing save Jesus Christ, and Him crucified', and, eschewing all worldly and carnal methods and devices, to rely upon the power of the Holy Spirit.

I need not appeal for your continued loyalty and support: I thank God for it as you have shown it in every realm. May I ask that members will be careful to place their cards in the offering plate at the Communion Service, as this is our only means of registering attendance. If obliged to be absent, it would be appreciated if the cards could be sent in by post, or through the offering plate at any service.

We have been happy to welcome home during the year several of our members who had served with the Forces during the war. We rejoice that their faith has remained undimmed, and that several of them have resumed their old tasks with renewed zeal and vigour. Our warmest greetings go out to those who are still serving and to all who are prevented by circumstances from meeting with us regularly.

'Now the God of hope fill you with all joy and peace in believing, that ye may abound in hope, through the power of the Holy Ghost.'

I am,

Yours in the bonds of Christ,

      D. M. Lloyd-Jones

Annual Letter, 1948

Westminster Chapel,
Buckingham Gate,
London S.W.1
January, 1948

[To the Members of Westminster Chapel]

Dear Friend,

Once more it is my privilege at the beginning of a New Year to send you a word of greeting in the name of Christ.

I avail myself of the opportunity readily and gladly, because in a church like ours where it is so difficult to maintain the personal touch, it does provide an opportunity for something more intimate than the usual relationship between pulpit and pew. The feeling uppermost within me is one of thankfulness to God for all His graciousness throughout another year. He has been pleased to grant us seasons of refreshing, and once more we thank Him for working again the miracle of redeeming grace in our midst. We likewise welcome the many friends who have come into the membership of the church during the past year. We know already that they have brought a blessing with them, and we are happy in the thought that what has brought them amongst us has been the fact that they had been conscious of blessing, when worshipping with us.

I cannot hope to express my sense of deep gratitude to God for all who have so faithfully supported and helped in the work in so many ways. The generosity shown in time, energy and money has been truly remarkable.

As we face the future with all its uncertainties it seems more and more clear that Westminster Chapel has been set here in the very heart of London to bear witness to the great evangelical faith and tradition. It is a humbling and yet stimulating and challenging thought that there are many scattered about these islands and indeed in other lands who are looking to us and are helped and strengthened by what we are and what we do. We may well ask, 'Who is sufficient for these things?' Yet our reply to the question, thank God, is certain and unequivocal, 'Our sufficiency is of God'.

We shall continue to 'declare the Lord's death until He come' as we are enabled, and as we are helped by your prayers and by 'your fellowship in the Gospel'.

My prayer is that God may continue to bless you and 'that thou mayest prosper and be in health even as thy soul prospereth'.

May 'the God of all grace, Who hath called us unto His eternal glory by Christ Jesus, after that ye have suffered a while, make you perfect, stablish, strengthen, settle you. To Him be glory and dominion for ever and ever. Amen.'

Yours in the bonds of Christ,

D. M. Lloyd-Jones

Annual Letter, 1953

Westminster Chapel,
Buckingham Gate,
London S.W.1
January, 1953

[To the Members of Westminster Chapel]
Dear Friend,

Another year has come and gone since last I addressed you in this particular way. Once more I count it a real privilege to send you this word of salutation, greeting and good cheer.

The one thing that I always regret more than anything else in our church life together is the fact that we are not able to have that intimate and personal contact that would give us all great joy.

Owing to the situation of our church building and the very nature of our church and witness, this is more or less inevitable. This letter, therefore, helps to maintain the link.

In spite of what I have just said, I am constantly being told of the real and happy fellowship which many find in the church and its life. Certainly, for myself, I am more and more conscious of this sense of a strong and growing fellowship. Often my heart is gladdened by observing, or hearing of, friendships that have sprung up amongst those who have found themselves sitting near one another in the services.

True fellowship, however, is 'in the Spirit', and, thank God, we can and do enjoy this though we may not actually speak to each other directly, for we have wonderful fellowship with one another as we enjoy our common fellowship 'with the Father and with His Son Jesus Christ'.

In this fellowship we can again unite in thanking God for another year in which we have experienced His gracious dealings with us and His loving encouragement. Speaking for myself I can say that I have never experienced greater joy and freedom in preaching. Above all, I would testify to a sense of being dealt with by God and a sense that we are all being prepared by Him for something unusual.

Missionary friends who have worshipped with us for some time and who have recently returned to their 'field' have frequently said that they felt that revival blessing was very near. God grant that this may be so, and may we all be urgent in prayer and supplication to that end. Surely it must be plain to all who are spiritually alive and alert that nothing else will suffice to stem the mounting tide of blatant and boastful godlessness and vice. A set, polite and formal religion is worse than useless. The clamant need of the hour is for men and women in whom our Lord and Saviour is glorified, and who are ready to be His witnesses, confessors, and, if necessary, martyrs.

It has been the greatest of all privileges to witness again the rebirth of numbers of souls, and it is with real joy that we have welcomed many into the full fellowship of the church. Friends have come among us from many and varied branches of the Christian church proving that the only true and real ecumenicity is that which is based upon a common understanding of the teaching of God's infallible word and a common love to our blessed Lord and Saviour Jesus Christ.

You will not desire or expect me to thank you for your faithfulness and your generosity in your material gifts to God's work. I would simply say that I am more and more amazed and encouraged.

Thus we enter 1953 grateful and hopeful, looking for 'the greater things' that our Lord always has for those who truly seek Him and obey Him.

Committing you to His loving care and to 'the word of His Grace which is able to build you up',

I remain,

Yours in His glorious service,

D. M. Lloyd-Jones

Annual Letter, 1954

Westminster Chapel,
Buckingham Gate,
London S.W.1
January, 1954

[To the Members of Westminster Chapel]

Dear Friend,

It is difficult to believe that another year has come and gone since last I had the privilege of addressing you in this way. Time passes so quickly, and is most certainly 'an ever-rolling stream'. It brings us along almost unconsciously, and we only realise what is happening when the end of the year or some special event in our lives makes us stop for a moment to consider.

More and more in connection with my work as your Minister, and in the life of our church, I have realised the importance of the exhortation given by the saintly William Chalmers Burns to a young minister: 'Brother, we must hurry.' The opportunities are endless, the need of men and women has never been greater.

[93]

I have certainly never known a more active and busy year in connection with the life of our fellowship. Neither have I known a more interesting, or indeed thrilling year. Never have I been more deeply conscious, of the high privilege of being the Minister of such a church. The many-sidedness of the work is quite astonishing.

The work of direct evangelism goes on regularly, and the histories and background of those brought to a saving faith in our Lord is quite astonishing. At one extreme are those who literally had no religious background whatsoever. At the other end are those who were brought up as Roman Catholics. The commonest type, however, consists of those who had always regarded themselves as good Christians, but who found after attending the services that they had never known the Truth at all. But, coming thus in various ways, they have all arrived at the same knowledge of our Lord and Saviour Jesus Christ.

More and more, also, at the same time, we seem to be attracting those who have spiritual problems. The confusion prevailing in the religious world is acute, with so many movements and ideas and special emphases. Added to this are problems and difficulties and perplexities of a more personal character. On top of all I am persuaded that Satan is unusually active these days, and is making a special onslaught on those who are most faithful. It is to me as great a joy to watch our Lord healing and restoring these, as it is to see Him saving the first group.

I say all this because I would have you know that you are in active participation in this work and ministry. You hold up my hands, and your faithfulness and prayers mean more than you can realise. I can but thank God for you and appeal to you to continue to bring with you all who have any kind of spiritual need.

We all rejoice together in those of our company who have heard and responded to the call of our Lord to service in other lands during the past year. It is a privilege to feel that they belong to us. Let us continue to remember them in our prayers.

Thus, while thanking God for all His goodness to us and all His gracious dealing with us, my profound conviction is that 'the best is yet to be'.

'Commending you to God and to the word of His grace which is able to build you up and to give you an inheritance among all them who are sanctified.'

I remain,

Yours in the Lord,

D. M. Lloyd-Jones

Annual Letter, 1957

Westminster Chapel,
Buckingham Gate,
London S.W.1
January, 1957

[To the Members of Westminster Chapel]

Dear Friend,

It is scarcely credible that a year has passed since I last sent you a word of greeting as your Minister and Pastor. But such is the case, and it is a joy and privilege to greet you once more in the name of our Lord and Saviour Jesus Christ.

This has been a remarkable year in many ways. Above everything else there stands out the consciousness of God's good hand upon us. This is shown not only in the size and steadiness of the congregations and the marvellous generosity shown by the free-will offerings Sunday by Sunday, but still more in an ever-deepening sense of the privilege and the glory of being 'Fellow-citizens with the Saints and of the household of God'. We praise God for all who have been convicted and converted by the Truth in our midst during the past year, but our praise is no less for the marked and evident signs of a process of deepening, both as regards understanding and experience, which are noticeable in so many. Growth and maturity are as much the work of God as birth, and a church which neglects this aspect does not conform to the New Testament pattern. I cannot imagine anything more uplifting and thrilling, and indeed exciting, than to try to follow the glowing mind and soaring spirit of the Apostle Paul, as we have been doing on Sunday mornings and Friday evenings in our studies of the

Epistles of the Ephesians and the Romans. We have not only been given to see that 'in Christ' we are 'seated together in the heavenly places', but at times even to feel it and to rejoice in it.

All this has been the inevitable effect of consolidating our sense of fellowship and of relationship to one another. Nothing gives me personally greater delight than this, and to hear frequent testimonial to it. Quite often visitors tell me that they are conscious of this in our services, and it has been almost pathetic at times to receive letters from friends from other countries, who have spent a year or two as Members of the Congregation, stating how greatly they have missed the friendship and the fellowship, even after returning to their home churches! In giving a special word of welcome and of greeting to those who have joined us during the past year, I would urge them to enter into all the various activities of the church 'behind the scenes' that they may enjoy the fellowship fully.

The past year saw the coming amongst us of Mr Iain Murray, B.A., to help in the work of the ministry. He has already settled happily amongst us and his devout spirit and teaching gift are much appreciated.

While thus enriched, we have suffered a great loss in the passing of Sister Dora, who, although in semi-retirement for the past two years, nevertheless continued to handle certain vital aspects of the work. She had rendered most loyal and devoted service to the church for nearly 50 years. I cannot praise too highly her personal loyalty and her meticulous accuracy and carefulness in all she did. These are the supreme virtues in anyone who serves the Lord in a secretarial capacity. We thank God for her, for all she did and for all she was, especially to 'the poor and needy'.

'Here have we no continuing city', but thank God, 'we seek one to come'. May He Who has promised 'never to leave us nor to forsake us' fill us all with 'all joy and peace in believing' during 1957 and always.

Yours in His glorious service,

D. M. Lloyd Jones

5

SOME FAMILY LETTERS

Removal to Ealing

The Haven,
Chatsworth Avenue,
Haslemere, Surrey
11 October, 1943

[To his Mother]
My Dear Mama,

Your letter written yesterday at Port Talbot has just arrived. We are very glad indeed to have had all your news and especially as to your whereabouts so that I know where to write to you.

You understand that as far as we are concerned there is no need for you to rush back until you are absolutely ready. The only work at the moment is the sewing in connection with the curtains and that is something which Bethan must do herself.[1] Actually she is progressing very rapidly with it and has broken the back of the job.

With Pickford doing the moving there is no other packing that one can do.

I had a good visit to Glasgow. We had the St. Andrew's Hall packed again on the Monday night and I enjoyed speaking there very much. We also had a good crowd at the service on the Tuesday night. I did not see the Allisons. I tried to find them in the telephone directory but completely failed to do so. I wrote to them last Thursday.

---

[1] They were shortly to move to 2 Colebrooke Avenue, Ealing, and in war-time conditions the ability to black-out all windows was a first necessity. In a previous letter he had told his mother: 'The black-out material has arrived and I helped Bethan to cut it out. It took a long time.'

I unfortunately caught a bit of cold on the return journey but it has not bothered me much. Indeed I was less tired after the two services yesterday at Westminster than I have been after one service only.[1]

By the way the attendances there and the collections have been good both Sundays – well ahead of last year. C. M. looks very well but he was complaining yesterday that his right leg is almost becoming useless. Poor Miss Howell has had to go into hospital for a few weeks' rest.

Our visit to Ealing last Wednesday was very satisfactory. Secrett has done the house himself beautifully. Ann and Elizabeth have been accepted at the schools. Ann will start the next half term and Elizabeth in January. Both are delighted. Ann returned to school here today. We are also having beautiful weather these days.

I have various odd meetings in London tomorrow. I stay tomorrow night with Mr and Mrs Secrett. I am to preach twice at Watford on Wednesday and hope to get back here on the 11.00 p.m. train that night.

Your very welcome parcel arrived dinner time today. All was perfect except that one of the eggs was hopelessly smashed! The butter of course I value particularly. I do not think Nellie's case is likely to be serious. We await news of poor Ianto Penrhos with much greater anxiety. His chances are poor. Emrys and Peggy have been really kind. It is very good of them. I think that is all I have to say.

Our fondest love to you my dear Mama,

Your loving son,

Martyn

---

[1] Dr Campbell Morgan had preached for the last time as co-pastor on the last Sunday morning in August. From that point ML-J took all services. His health was clearly much better than in the years immediately following his arrival at Westminster Chapel. Morgan died 16 May 1945. It was typical of ML-J that he kept material by his predecessor in the *Westminster Record* for at least ten years after his death.

Services and Rockets

2 Colebrooke Avenue,
Ealing, London W.13
23 October, 1944

[To his Mother]

My Dear Mama,

Many thanks for your short note last week and also for the *Welsh Gazette* which arrived this morning.

It was good to know that Uncle David is definitely out of danger. You did not seem to have any other particular news to give.

I much enjoyed my trip to Yorkshire last week. Ivor Thomas made an excellent host. I believe he is improving as the result of being in Parliament. We had an excellent meeting there, my fellow speaker being Dr Donald Soper.[1]

I preached twice in London on Wednesday – Bromley and Streatham. Again I preached in Mitcham on Saturday afternoon. Between everything I am having an exceptionally busy time. We had a good day again yesterday [at Westminster]. The morning congregations are really good these days but the evenings are poor. I am given to understand that the 6.00 p.m. is not taking well anywhere. We may consider changing it and having it at a slightly earlier hour.

The Friday night discussion meeting was started again at the beginning of this month and is also going quite well considering the black-out.[2] There were about 60 people there last Friday.

[1] This was a meeting at Keighley, arranged by Ivor Thomas, MP. At a later date ML-J would not have preached alongside a known liberal such as Soper.

[2] He placed much importance on this meeting which was designed for fellowship as well as instruction. Questions were taken up of a practical and spiritual nature and he sought to get the meeting to arrive at answers in terms of Scripture. See *D. Martyn Lloyd-Jones: The Fight of Faith*, pp. 167–75. With reluctance in 1952 he changed this meeting for a service in the main auditorium of the Chapel and commenced a series on 'Biblical Doctrines'. This was followed by his lectures on Romans (1955–68).

On the whole we are having a quiet time as regards bombing. The flying bombs never seem to get anywhere near here and the warnings only last about 1/4 hour. But at 1.30 a.m. on Saturday morning there was a terrific explosion from one of those rocket bombs. It shook the house and we knew it was not very far away. Actually it was at Hayes, which as you know, is just beyond Hanwell. One had fallen in South Norwood at 8.20 Friday evening, but we did not hear that. Their noise is terrible and unlike the flying bombs they make deep craters and do not spread so much.

I am just off to Manchester. I shall stay tonight with the Rev. and Mrs D. L. Rees. I preach in Manchester at 12.45 p.m. tomorrow, then I go to Rhyl where I am due to preach for Mr Edward Williams on Tuesday and Wednesday evenings. Back home on Thursday in time for Elizabeth's birthday tea, D.V.

Let us know your news.

Our fondest love to you my dear Mama and love to Mr and Mrs Edgar,

Your loving son,

Martyn

Visit to Norway

39 Mount Park Crescent,
Ealing, London W.5
20 September, 1946

[To his Mother]
My Dear Mama,

Well, you will see that I am safely back again.

We were glad to get your letter and all the news. It was here when Elizabeth and I got back on Wednesday night. I had to go and preach that afternoon and evening at Haywards Heath. Elizabeth came to meet again the people with whom she had been staying and working at Borth in the summer.

The news about poor Gladys is of course what one expected, but if she is really jaundiced as you suggest it means that her disease has already spread into her liver. That again means it is advancing very rapidly.

I was truly sorry to hear what you said about poor Dai Rich.[1] For some reason or other I had not seen him since the war of 1914–18 and had not heard anything about him for years. It is a real tragedy. That poor girl his wife has known much trouble in her life.

I am not surprised to hear of the death of Dr Wilson as I know that he had to retire on account of his heart some time ago. Strange though that he should have died at Porthcawl.

Well, we arrived back on Monday. I should have been here first were it not that my train was very late. Actually they got here about half an hour before me.[2] Mrs Emlyn Davies met them at Paddington with a car according to our arrangements, so all was well.

As for myself I cannot begin to give you an account of my visit to Norway. I enjoyed it immensely. The voyage over was absolutely perfect. The weather was glorious and I did not miss a single meal.

I was given quite a reception and excellent crowds turned up at all my meetings. There was no need for an interpreter as they understood my English quite easily. The scenery is beautiful. I shall never forget my journey from Oslo to Bergen on the Friday. It took over 12 hours. At one station we were 3,662 feet above sea level – higher than Snowdon. There was snow of course on the mountains. Norway is really Scotland on a very very much larger scale. It also reminded me very forcibly of Canada – northern Ontario especially. The houses are made of wood and the rock is to be seen through the earth everywhere. I should say that the very best farming there was about the worst in Wales. The cattle seemed much the same as ours – shorthorn chiefly. The horses were really poor. I did not see a single shire – they seemed to be a cross between colliers and ponies.

[1] Dafydd Richards.
[2] The family had been in Wales while he was in Norway.

As regards food, clothing, things in shops and prices, they seemed to be almost exactly as we are in this country. They had a terrible time under the Germans, but now they are full of fear of the Russians and expecting them to walk in.

Unfortunately we ran into a gale on the way back. I woke up in the middle of the night on Saturday feeling sick. Sunday all day I did not get up at all. I tried to be sick three times but failed on Sunday morning. After that I was all right except that I had pain in my stomach. Only five people had lunch on the Sunday! It was really rough. I have never seen such waves before. I still feel a little giddy and light-headed after it.

Well, there is no other special news. Look after yourself and keep warm and if you cannot, come back at once.

Our fondest love to you my dear Mama and love to all,

Your loving son,

Martyn

Crossing the Atlantic Again

'Empress of Canada'
22 July, 1947

[To his Mother][1]

My dear Mama,

We are now almost within six hours of arriving at Quebec and as we are told that we shall be able to send off letters by air-mail from there I thought I would write you a word. This is the first I have written since I sent you the letter-card from Liverpool last Wednesday.

You will be glad to know that we have had an excellent trip across. The sea has been as calm as it was when we crossed in the 'Berengaria' ten years ago. Naturally I have thought a lot of that time and of the various things that happened to us. You should have been with us this time. It seems to me that Ann is your true

---

[1] The first of four letters written to his mother on his third visit to North America.

descendant and representative. She enters into everything and enjoys every moment exactly as you did. She has made me think of you many many times. She seems to know everybody and to be friendly with everyone. She is certainly a very good mixer and Bethan and I agree that she undoubtedly gets it directly from you!

Well now let me try to give you some details of the trip.

I told you that we had received your telegram before leaving. What a day it was! We eventually left dock at 10.00 p.m. There were of course no people standing on the quay to see anybody off. I must say that that detracts a good deal from the pleasure and the greatness of the occasion. All the excitement and thrill are removed.[1] It will be good when all this fuss about currency comes to an end.

When I went to the Purser's office I found at once that the assistant-Purser obviously recognised me and clearly had a Welsh accent. He came down with me to the cabin and told me that I must not stand in a queue for anything and that he will deal with all my affairs. He turned out to be a man by the name of Jones from Aberayron, and a nephew of our neighbour G. W. Evans, 40 Mount Park Crescent! He is a nice little fellow who now lives in Liverpool and had of course heard me preach there many times. He told me this morning that if he had been Purser and not assistant that I would have had to preach last Sunday evening! He dealt with all my affairs with the Immigration people this morning and he tells me that he will get us through the Customs at Montreal tomorrow without any delay. Thus again I have proved what a real advantage it is to be a Welshman!

We have a very nice cabin with just three bunks. It is long and airy and roomy and we have all slept well. The food has been first-class, indeed pre-war. We cannot get over the whiteness of the bread. Ann, of course, has been rejoicing in the ice-cream.

The only day when we felt at all ill was Thursday and especially at night when it became choppy. Ann was sick once in the

[1] The emotion stirred by ocean-going liners departing for other shores has now passed into history. For multitudes, both departing and staying, it was an unforgettable experience.

morning and didn't take any dinner that night. Bethan and I haven't missed a single meal. Quite suddenly on Thursday night about two hours after dinner and without any warning at all I was suddenly sick. It was all over in a minute and I slept well and have been all right ever since.

We have just one lady with us at our table. On hearing that her name was Mrs Loughborough I asked if she by any chance knew a man of that name who was an X-ray doctor at Barts. It turned out that she is his sister-in-law. I knew him very well indeed. She was most pleased and excited at this.

On Sunday we were talking to a man in the lounge and, on finding that he and his sister-in-law were attending a religious conference at Buffalo, Bethan told the lady that I was at Westminster Chapel. The moment the man heard this he asked, 'But where is Dr Jones Martyn now then?'. He had heard of me many times. I knew a great friend of his at Manchester. What a small world it is after all.

We picked up the pilot at 7.00 a.m. this morning. We are due at Quebec about 5.00 p.m. this afternoon and due to land at Montreal tomorrow morning about 10.00 a.m. Unfortunately there is a thick mist so we can see nothing just now.

We finished with the land in North Ireland last Thursday morning and then saw none until yesterday morning (Monday) when we had Newfoundland to the south of us and Labrador to the north. By now I take it you are with the good friends at Corwen. Please give them my warm regards and tell them I still have happy recollections of my stay with them eight years ago. I hope too that you are feeling rested by now and enjoying the change. Do look after yourself. Bethan and Ann join me in sending our fondest love to you my dear Mama.

Ever your loving son,
    Martyn

Her Birthday

39 Mount Park Crescent,
Ealing, London W.5
13 January, 1947

[To his Mother]
My dear Mama,

As we are to see you tomorrow afternoon I just write this hurried note with the enclosed to wish you many happy returns of the day.

You know all I would say. As the years pass and as friends of long-standing are taken one after another we learn to value increasingly the closest and dearest ties here on earth.

God has been very good to us as a family and we thank Him for it.

We all join together in our fondest love and we look forward to tomorrow afternoon.

Ever your loving son,
Martyn

True Christianity

39 Mount Park Crescent,
Ealing, London W.5
17 May, 1948

[To his Mother]
My dear Mama,

Just a word with the *Welsh Gazette* before I leave for Swanwick in Derbyshire where I have to speak tonight and twice tomorrow.

We were glad to get your letter and to know that you are having an excellent time. With the glorious weather it must be still better. Your time there must be coming to an end. What are your further plans. Let us know.

Glad to say that we are all right here except that Ann has a bit of a cold in the head but nothing much. There is no special news.

The Friday night meeting was down in attendance as large numbers of people are away for the week-end [Whitsun holiday]. The Rowlandsons were not there. It was quite a good discussion.[1]

Yesterday to my amazement we had full congregations quite up to our usual standard. There were large numbers of visitors of course to make up for our absent people.

In the morning I preached on Philippians 4:4 shewing how nothing but our belief in the Lord Jesus Christ can make us happy 'always'.[2] Everything else must fail us sooner or later, but this never.

Last night I preached on Acts 18:24–28 especially on Apollos. I described him and what a wonderful man he was, with his Jewish faith and Greek culture as learned in Alexandria, and how eloquent he was and how he preached the same message as John the Baptist. But Aquila and his wife Priscilla, who were ordinary people and just tentmakers, saw that he was lacking in the true Christian message and took him aside and told him what he did not know about the death of Christ and its meaning, the resurrection and the descent of the Holy Ghost on the Day of Pentecost at Jerusalem.

Though he was such a great man he was humble enough to listen to them and to believe what they said. And it entirely changed his message and made a new man of him. Anything short of preaching that Christ is the Son of God and that His death and resurrection save us is not true Christianity.

Well, my dear Mama continue to enjoy yourself. Please convey our love to your kind and good host.

Our fondest love to you my dear Mama,

Ever your loving,

Martyn

[1] His mother attended Westminster Chapel when in London and was a member. On her death (22 June 1951) a short tribute was placed by the Church Secretary, Mr A. E. Marsh, in the *Westminster Record*. He spoke of her as 'overflowing with sympathy and kindness for others ... "interested in everyone and everything," and never happier than when seeking to know why any member of the church was absent and to enquire after his or her welfare.'

[2] Published in *The Life of Peace* (London: Hodder and Stoughton, 1990), pp. 141–52.

A First Visit to Donegal

Rosapenna Hotel,
Co. Donegal
5 September, 1949

[To his Mother]

My dear Mama,

Your letter from Dolgian[1] and the enclosed letter from John to Bethan and the *Goleuad* arrived safely this morning. We were glad to hear that you have arrived safely at Dolgian and that you are having a good time there. We knew that you would. It is such a pity that your bladder is still giving you trouble. Please send Dr Ker's prescription home for me to see it or else get the chemist down there to make a copy which I can see. The sample for which I sent must be about arriving now and if you think it will not disagree with what Dr Ker is giving you I will send it on to you.

We have had a wonderful holiday here. The services on the two Sundays were well attended and in every way satisfactory.

The scenery here is truly wonderful. The mountains and the lakes and the sea are all excellent. But it is very sad to see the poverty of the people. How they manage to maintain any kind of health in the cottages or rather hovels in which they live I do not know. Of course the land round here is very poor indeed because it is so rocky. The only place in Wales of which the scenery reminds me at all is parts of Pembrokeshire especially round Treffgarne Rocks.

We have heard several times from the girls at Eastbourne and they seem to be enjoying themselves very much indeed. They are due to arrive home on Wednesday. They will stay Wednesday night with Mr and Mrs Harris (Pamela's people). Bethan and I are due to leave here on Wednesday afternoon and we hope to be home by about 1.00 p.m. on Thursday. We shall be motored to Belfast and then by sea to Heysham.

[1] A farm of her brother Bob's at Brongest, Newcastle Emlyn, and the area of childhood.

It will be strange to be home again after so long an absence and especially to have to start working once more. I hear that Scroggie[1] has had good congregations and that all is well at Westminster. Please give our love to all down there and let us know of your movements and plans and arrangements.

Bethan and I join in fondest love to you my dear Mama,

Ever your loving son,

Martyn

Holiday in Switzerland

Adelboden,
27 August, 1950

[To his Mother]

My dear Mama,

At last there is a little leisure for writing. We were very glad to get your letter when we arrived here on Friday night and to know that you were at any rate on your way to Cardiganshire.

We have seen great sights during this past week, indeed never to be forgotten. Monday we spent sight-seeing in Venice. Fortunately the heat was not too great so we were able to enjoy it. We were taken to see a glass factory where some of the finest vases are made. The great cathedral is, of course, also wonderful.

We set off on Tuesday morning in sweltering heat but we soon reached the mountain passes and it got cooler. We spent the night at a road-side hotel which was just under 6,000 feet above sea level. It was right on its own in the mountains with a stream tumbling down outside. There was a great mountain with its peak covered with snow just outside. Wednesday we set off again and crossed two great mountain ranges with most wonderful scenery until we arrived at the Swiss border and then ran on to St. Moritz. We saw a most wonderful glacier just before we reached St. Moritz. I was not very impressed with St. Moritz – I prefer the smaller places

[1] Dr W. Graham Scroggie, Scottish Baptist, one of the men supplying the pulpit during ML-J's vacation.

in the country. After leaving St. Moritz and climbing another mountain pass, as we were descending the other side our car broke down. We were able to glide into a little village called Bivio fortunately and found a very nice little hotel there. The garage man found that something had gone wrong with our water cooling system and that he would have to send for a spare part to Zurich. So we spent the whole of Thursday there. It was very delightful. Our hotel itself was about 5,500 feet above sea level. The food was really excellent and we went for a walk into the mountains in the afternoon and enjoyed ourselves very much indeed. Even Ann is beginning to appreciate scenery at last and she has taken a large number of photographs.

The spare part arrived on Thursday night by express delivery, so we were able to continue our journey on Friday morning. In many ways from the scenery standpoint that was our best day. We went to a place called Chur and then over the Oberalp pass to Andermatt. During the whole of that we were running up the valley of the river Rhine and arrived within a few miles of its source. At Andermatt we turned north and then crossed one of the newest and latest passes called the Susten pass. The scenery was really glorious and we saw a whole series of glaciers and great mountains. We got down to Meiringen and from there to Interlaken. From there we went south to Lauterbrunnen and then to see the famous Trummelbach water-falls. I certainly think these falls are one of the greatest sights in the world. Then we went back to Interlaken and on here arriving about 8.30 p.m. Yesterday we went up in the little carriage that goes up the mountain to the top and had the view. In the afternoon we just walked about the town etc. We went to the English Church this morning and are now off to Interlaken for an evening service and also to see Spietz. Tomorrow we leave in the morning and hope to see Bern on our way back into France. We are to spend tomorrow night at Troyes. On Tuesday we hope to travel to Paris. Wednesday is to be spent in Paris and that night we are to cross home and hope to arrive about 9.00 on Thursday.

I leave for the Conference at Cambridge on Thursday evening and Bethan and Ann will come on Friday night. My address at

Cambridge will be: c/o Tyndale House, Selwyn Rd, Cambridge.

I thought much yesterday of 28 years ago. It is almost incredible to believe that such a long time has passed since that day.[1]

I do hope you are resting as much as you can.

Bethan and the girls join me in fondest love to you my dear Mama and love to all down there.

Ever your loving son,
Martyn

Conference in Cambridge

Cambridge,
10 September, 1950

[To his Mother]
My Dear Mama,

I am truly sorry that I have not been able to write to you earlier than this, but it has really been a most exceptionally busy time.[2] I do not know that I have ever had a fuller week. We have been hard at it from morning to night. The programme has been roughly this. We were called at 6.45 a.m. for Prayers in the Chapel [of Ridley College] at 7.30. Breakfast at 8.00. Then I had a committee meeting each morning straight after breakfast. The first regular meeting was at 9.30, the next at 11.30. Then each afternoon after lunch there was generally a committee meeting except Wednesday when we all went on a bus to see Ely cathedral and Huntingdon. Then tea at 4.00. Another meeting at 5.00. Dinner at 7.00, and another meeting at 8.00. Then a final cup of coffee and bed.

---

[1] The anniversary of his father's death in 1922. His special thought of his mother at such times was characteristic.

[2] The second General Committee Meeting of the International Fellowship of Evangelical Students which met at Tyndale House and Ridley Hall, 2–9 September, and was preceded by a meeting of the Executive Committee.

You will see that it really has been a very full week and we are all feeling somewhat tired. We are leaving for home on the 9.27 a.m. train tomorrow (Monday). There have been delegates here from 22 countries, so it has been very interesting.

Unfortunately the weather has been very cold on the whole and the beds here are not too comfortable. But the food has been really good and that has been a very great help. Ann and Elizabeth have enjoyed themselves very much. Ann went to London yesterday to the re-union meetings of the camp to which she had been. She is spending the week-end with Mrs [Winifred] Secrett and Ruth until we get back tomorrow.

We were glad to get your card from Llandrindod on Tuesday and we got into touch with Nelian that evening. We shall hear from you as to when you returned to Dolgian and as to how Uncle Tom is progressing.

Naturally we have no real news to give you. Mr and Mrs [A. G.] Secrett were going away for their further holiday yesterday.

It seems a long time since we left for Ireland in July. We shall have to settle down again soon to the winter's work. I hope you have found all well down there and that you yourself are able to rest and benefit by the change. It is a pity that the weather has been so bad this summer.

I have an Induction Service at a place just outside Birmingham on Wednesday night but shall return home early on Thursday morning. Elizabeth will be studying I believe on Wednesday.

Please give our love to all down there. Our fondest love to you my dear Mama,

Your ever loving son,

Martyn

The first 'Weekly Report' to the Newly-Weds

39 Mount Park Crescent,
Ealing, London W.5
29 March, 1954

[Mr & Mrs H. F. R. Catherwood][1]
My Dear Fred and Elizabeth,

I cannot tell you the joy it gives me to write that for the first time. I look forward to repeating it week by week as regularly as I can.

We have been thinking about you constantly as you have been spending your first week in your own home. It was good to hear the other evening that you are getting straight. I thought of you especially yesterday morning and of how you would be leaving your home together for the first time to go to worship God.

I must try to give you some kind of a report on my doings since we saw you a week last night. On Tuesday I went to Barry to preach for Paul Tucker's church. We had two excellent congregations and I experienced liberty in preaching both afternoon and evening. In the afternoon I preached on the incident in Mark 8:22–26. At night, I preached on our Lord's handling of the Woman of Samaria. I felt there was real conviction in the evening service and so did Paul Tucker. He and his wife are very happy and have a nice home. I much enjoyed staying with them and I was particularly glad to hear what they said about Duncan Campbell[2] who had been staying with them recently. I had not realised before that he had a very special experience of the Holy Spirit in his life just before he went to the Hebrides. His analysis of evangelicalism in England is almost precisely mine.

---

[1] Elizabeth Lloyd-Jones had married Mr H. F. R. Catherwood ('Fred') in February 1954 and they were now settled in their first home at Gosforth, Newcastle-on-Tyne.

[2] The Rev. Duncan Campbell (1898–1972), United Free Church of Scotland and Faith Mission. A little is said of the experience referred to here in Andrew Wolsey, *Duncan Campbell – A Biography* (London: Hodder and Stoughton, 1974), pp. 97–8.

We all went to hear Dr Paul Rees at the Chapel on Thursday afternoon.[1] He was very good indeed on Elijah's mantle. He is a truly spiritual man and an effective speaker ... In the evening we had a church meeting with Caiger giving the usual financial report. It was a good meeting as he cut down his report to thirty minutes. What impressed and pleased me most was the fact that in 1953 we had given as a church the sum of £2,700 to home and foreign missionary work. The main chapel account was between £6,000 and £7,000.

On Friday night I was speaking on the biblical doctrine of faith. I shall send on Miss Human's typed notes when they arrive. It will probably be easier for you than struggling with my writing. I felt that there was unusual freedom in the meeting. I think the discerning were thinking in terms of Harringay.[2]

E. T. Rees of Port Talbot was there. He had been to the Free Church Federal Council annual meetings at Worthing. He came down to dinner on Saturday night and stayed until about 10.15. He is quite unchanged and regaled us with endless stories of our days in Aberavon and of the various characters. It was good to see him.

Yesterday we had two very large congregations, surprisingly large in view of the fact that the students are away on vacation. In the morning I preached on Romans 8:15–17. Here again I had better not give you my outline as Miss Leslie Thompson takes excellent notes and Miss Human types them out. I shall send them on to you. The essence of my message was the danger of being depressed and discouraged and in a state of bondage through turning the Christian life into a new kind of law.[3] The antidote is the

---

1 Dr Billy Graham's first London campaign was currently taking place at Harringay and Paul Rees took a series of meetings at Westminster Chapel for ministers and Christian workers.

2 Faith is *more* than our taking a decision.

3 'It is the failure of our faith to appropriate what is true of us in Christ ... holiness becomes a great task and we begin to plan and organise our lives in order to attain unto it' (MS sermon notes on Romans 8:15–17). The whole sermon can be found in *Spiritual Depression: Its Causes and*

full realisation of the doctrine of the Holy Spirit. He is within us in all His power (see v. 13) and also His presence reminds us of our relationship to God who is our Father.

Last night I preached on Exodus 3:16. This is the last of a series of six sermons on that chapter. You Elizabeth heard the first the Sunday before the wedding. The theme last night was this: Why do people not experience and enjoy the great salvation which God has provided? The answer is that their attitude is wrong, as it was with Moses at first. The initial attitude is impersonal, detached, external. It is curious and speculative and analytical. But God addressed Moses and the latter's attitude became entirely changed. How?

(1) It became personal – 'Moses, Moses'. We are not detached observers of God and religion. God is not a matter for theorising but a Person.

(2) It became reverent and full of fear. It is our ignorance of God that accounts for our attitude. It is true of us as Christians. We know little of trembling before God as the men of the Bible did and as others have done since. We do not realise the greatness and the majesty of God and His holiness as we should.

(3) He then began to listen instead of investigating.

(4) He submitted himself to the revelation though he did not understand it. He trusted God and His power. We must do the same.

(5) He acted on it.

I felt again that there was much conviction. But I long for the days when people will be broken down.

At the close of the evening service among others who came to see me was Sheila Williams, your old pupil Elizabeth. She is becoming a member of the church. A grand-daughter of Keri Evans is also joining, also from Llanelli. For Fred's sake I had better not say what Sheila said about you Elizabeth and what the school thought of you.

Cure (London: Pickering and Inglis, 1965). It was not, of course, part of his full exposition of Romans which began in October 1955 and ran to March 1968.

I must stop otherwise we shall miss the post. Mrs Catherwood is coming down to spend the evening with us. Ann and Carol Saunders have gone to the Old Vic to see Coriolanus. I go to Birmingham to preach twice – a service in English arranged by the Welsh community.

Our fondest love to you both,

Ever your loving,

Father

More News. On Seeking 'Full Assurance'

39 Mount Park Crescent,
Ealing, London W.5
5 April, 1954

[To Mr & Mrs H. F. R. Catherwood]

My dear Fred and Elizabeth,

As we told you we were truly delighted to hear your voices on the telephone on Friday night. At the same time we heartily approve of your most wise decision to concentrate on writing to thank all the various people who so kindly gave you presents.

I must now try to give you some account of my doings. I went to Birmingham on Tuesday and preached to a congregation called together by the Welsh community. I preached on the Woman of Samaria. I was amazed myself how readily it lent itself to the occasion as the condition of the Samaritans was so similar to that of modern Wales – Nationalism, interest in religion and theology and preaching etc., and yet ignorance of the gospel in any living and vital sense. I felt I was given much liberty and authority.

We all went to hear Dr Paul Rees last Thursday afternoon. I was beginning to think that your assessment of him last summer, Elizabeth, is probably right. But he is a very nice and a very good man. I addressed a meeting of the stewards at 6.30 p.m. and was interested to see Malcolm Hennell amongst them.

The Friday night meeting was in many ways quite outstanding. I spoke on Assurance of Faith and went on until between 7.45 and 7.50! The main cause of this was my exposition of Romans 8:16. I hold the view that the R.S.V. translation is quite wrong. It says, 'When we cry, "Abba! Father!" it is the Spirit bearing witness with our spirit that we are the children of God.' I think that is quite wrong and that this refers to a special direct witness of the Spirit *with* not *to* our spirit. It is additional to the spirit of adoption.[1] It is the type of experience that Wesley had and Whitefield and Jonathan Edwards and Finney and Moody.[2] I believe that the absence of this is the main cause of our poor spiritual lives.

I was really dealing with this once more yesterday morning when I preached on Ephesians 3:14–21 especially with 'that Christ may dwell in your hearts by faith'. This is 'knowing His love' and not ordinary Christian experience. It is the conscious realisation of Christ within us and the present knowledge of His love to us. It is the norm for Christians and we must seek it until we have it. I believe that the Keswick teaching is particularly wrong just here. It says: 'Surrender and accept by faith. Do not worry about your

[1] His point is that Romans 8:16 is not simply an explanation of v. 15 (and so not to be conflated with v. 16 as the R.S.V. translation), rather v. 16 is more than the Spirit's testimony to our conscience of our sonship; it is additional to that, a concurrent witness 'with' our spirit. For full exposition see his *Romans: Exposition of Chapter 8:5–17* (Edinburgh: Banner of Truth, 1974), pp. 285–399, being sermons preached in 1960–61. It is important to note that what ML-J is discussing is *assurance* of salvation. When his teaching on this subject became more widely discussed in the 1960s some represented it as a novelty, but historic evangelical Christianity had never taught that full or 'infallible' assurance was common to all regenerate persons. See *The Westminster Confession of Faith*, Chapter xvii: 3.

[2] See Wesley, *Sermons on Several Occasions* (London, 1824), vol. 1, Sermon xi, 'The Witness of the Spirit'; *George Whitefield's Journals* (London: Banner of Truth, 1960), pp. 58–59); *Jonathan Edwards: A New Biography*, Iain H. Murray (Edinburgh: Banner of Truth, 1987), pp. 99–100; *The Memoirs of Charles G. Finney: The Complete Restored Text*, ed. G. M. Rosell and R. A. G. Dupuis (Grand Rapids: Zondervan, 1989), p. 23; *The Life of Dwight L. Moody*, W. R. Moody (London: Morgan and Scott, n.d.), p. 135. This is not, of course, to say that ML-J agreed with the way all these men formulated their teaching on such experiences. See *D. Martyn Lloyd-Jones: The Fight of Faith*, pp. 383, 386, 484–85, 487, 662.

feelings; believe that you have it.' But the experiences of the men to whom I have referred do not agree with that. The experience they had was overwhelming, not a matter of persuading themselves but of being so filled with the love of God that like Moody they had to ask God to desist lest their very bodies might collapse under the glory. So I emphasised the fact that Paul's first petition was that God would '*grant*' that experience to us. It is His gift. The first thing we need is to be strengthened by the power of the Spirit in the inner man, otherwise we cannot contain it. Above all we must go on seeking it and longing for it and praying for it until we have it. It is clear that Paul expects *all* Christians to have this.

Last night I preached on Acts 17:1–3. My theme in general was this: Paul did not discuss the questions of the day but always preached Jesus. His method is important. It is not first an appeal but he 'reasoned', 'opened', 'alleged'. In other words, it was a declaration of truth in terms of the Old Testament revelation. He 'opened' the Scriptures, then reasoned in them and then alleged or propounded his message that Jesus is the Christ. It is the most momentous news of all. This is the message for today, not the H-bomb or anything else. For H-bomb or not we all have to die and to meet God and if we are reconciled to Him we are not afraid of the H-bomb or anything else. The H-bomb will simply usher us immediately into the presence of Christ. We do not invite people to become Christians to save the world from war or communism or bombs or anything else, but to save themselves from the wrath of God and perdition.

Ann and Elizabeth Braund maintain that it was an outstanding service. I was certainly conscious of being given power and authority.

My engagements this month are in and around London fortunately. There is nothing particular to report here. We have the 'at-home' meeting at Westminster on Thursday. I think I shall speak D.V. on systems of church government.

We all join in sending our fondest love,

Ever your loving,

Father

Preaching, Lecturing on Church Polity, and Romans 6:2 — 'The most important sermon I ever preached'

39 Mount Park Crescent,
Ealing, London W.5
12 April, 1954

[To Mr & Mrs H. F. R. Catherwood]
My Dear Fred and Elizabeth,

We were very glad to receive your letter Elizabeth and to have some more detailed account of your home and your doings. You are evidently most happy and having a busy time.

We now look forward eagerly to next week when we shall see you and see your home for the first time. The thought of doing so is quite exciting. We have not quite decided as yet where we shall stay on the Monday night but I am toying in my mind with the idea of Harrogate. I have never been there and I should like to see the place. We do not propose to reach you until after lunch on the Tuesday, so that you may have time to settle in properly after your week-end.

Now, some kind of report of the past week. I went with the Gilbeys on Tuesday evening to a little chapel at which Gilbey preaches occasionally and preached to 35 people. I always find such an occasion a real challenge and I believe I gave them of my best. I certainly enjoyed the service myself.

On Wednesday afternoon I preached at Greenford County Grammar School. They have four services each year and this was their Easter service. I was allowed 15 minutes but took 20! I took as my theme — why is Good Friday called 'Good' Friday? It appears to be such a bad day, why therefore is it called 'good'? I found it was a very good and convenient way of preaching the gospel. The 550 children, masters and mistresses, and the local clergy and ministers who had been invited, listened very well.

On Thursday we had our at-home at the Chapel. Slightly less than the usual number seemed to be present, nevertheless we were kept busy shaking hands for an hour. Upstairs in the Institute Hall I gave an address on Church Polity. I described the R.C.,

Anglican, Presbyterian, Independent, Baptist, Methodist, Quaker and Brethren positions. It was almost entirely factual and I did not argue the merits or demerits of the various views. As it was, it took me a full hour. I took it historically and therefore thoroughly enjoyed myself.

On Friday night I tried to deal with the doctrine of justification by faith only. I felt that I did not do it justice, largely due to the fact that I was somewhat tired physically. I shall send you the notes when they arrive. The main point emphasised was that faith is but the *instrument* of our justification, *not* the *grounds*. We are not justified *because* of our faith or on account of it. It is but the channel or instrument by which we receive the righteousness of our Lord by which we are justified. *He* is our justification, not our faith in Him. You will realise that many, if not most evangelicals these days, go astray at that point. It is a most subtle heresy which turns faith into a work and really teaches justification by works again, our faith being the works.

Yesterday morning I preached what I regard as the most important sermon I ever preached.[1] The text was Romans 6:2, but that then illustrated by chapters 5, 6, and 7, as 'the true view of our Lord's death'. I am not sure whether Miss Leslie Thompson was there or not so that you may have her notes. My points were these:

We cannot understand His death apart from the idea of the Covenant and our union with Him. We are given to Him by the Father (see John 17:2 etc.). We are in Him. All that happened to Him happened to us. We *were* crucified with Him, died with Him, were buried with Him, rose with Him, are seated with Him in the heavenly places. He is not only our federal head but we are united to Him, baptised *into* Him.

---

[1] It was crucial to him because up until this point he had been uncertain how to handle Romans 6: 'I suddenly felt that I had arrived at a satisfactory understanding' (*D. Martyn Lloyd-Jones: The Fight of Faith*, p. 639). It is typical of his balance that at the very period when he was speaking so strongly of the need for personal experience of the Holy Spirit he regarded the objective fact of the believer's union with Christ as absolutely foundational to a true understanding of the Christian life. Some were failing to arrive at true joy and peace because they failed to see the 'need to pray less and to think more' (*Spiritual Depression*, p. 173).

From all that Paul draws these deductions: We have died to sin (verse 20). Our old man is crucified with Him (verse 6); we have been crucified unto the world and the world unto us (Gal. 6:4); we are dead (Coloss. 3:3).

Then I made these assertions: It is entirely wrong to call upon us to crucify ourselves. Many do this. They say: 'Christ has died for you, now you must submit and die and be crucified with Him.' That is wrong because that has already happened. It happened on the cross. And because of that death, we have died to sin, to Satan and to the world. That means that the old Adamic man we were is no longer in existence. And so sin, Satan and the world have nothing to do with us. They cannot touch us as we do not belong to them (see 1 John 5:19 etc.). But we still sin. How? Paul's answer is in Romans 7:17 and 20 – it is no longer *I* that do it but sin that dwelleth in me. I am free from sin but what he calls the body of sin, in 6:6, remains. It is a kind of relic of sin ⸻ [indecipherable] in our bodies, in our members. That is why Paul looks forward to the redemption of the body so much.

The way to conquer sin and temptation is to realise all this – 6:11. We must not allow a relic of the old to control us, who are new men in Christ, we must realise that we no longer belong to that realm at all. And of course we are risen with Christ and have that new life and the Holy Spirit dwelling within us.

I trust that is fairly clear.

Last night I preached on Acts 17:3 – 'that Christ must needs have suffered'. It was a particularly large congregation and people felt that there was much conviction in the service.

You will be sorry to know that poor Miss Maunder is dangerously ill with heart failure in hospital. Mamgee is most grateful for the flowers that arrived safely on Saturday.

Your mother says Elizabeth that you must take an evening dress to Rosapenna.[1] Will you telephone to let us know which you

---

[1] Rosapenna Hotel, Donegal, owned by Fred's parents, and which Elizabeth's parents had visited in 1949 and 1953. ML-J was himself anticipating another visit to Rosapenna, where golf was a main occupation of guests, hence the light-hearted reference with which the letter closes.

would like us to send on to you if necessary. You will have a delightful week-end at Rosapenna I am sure. I am now reading Sam Snead's golfing lessons in the *Evening Standard* daily.

Our fondest love to you both,

Your ever loving,

Father

6

A YOUNGER GENERATION AND NEW AGENCIES

The Work in Wales

39 Mount Park Crescent,
Ealing, London W.5
8 March, 1949

[To Mr Elwyn Davies][1]
Dear Mr Elwyn Davies,

I am truly grateful for your very kind letter, and for the enclosure. I am particularly happy to hear the report concerning the effects and results of the Mission. I am sure that the work will continue to progress and to deepen. I was certainly conscious at the time that something very definite was happening.

With regard to the proposed meeting of ministers and students, I still feel, as I explained to the Rev. W. H. Davies last year, that what is needed is more a Conference than a Summer School. What I suggest is that men amongst ourselves be asked to read short opening papers on various subjects, and that we then discuss them together. In that way we can all profit by sharing our experiences and decide and determine policy.

With regard to dates. I am due at Ammanford on Wednesday, September 28th and Carmarthen on Thursday, September 29th. I could travel down on Monday the 26th and be present at a evening

[1] Elwyn Davies was a student in preparation for the Congregational ministry in Wales, and president of the Evangelical Union in Bangor University College where ML-J had shared in a mission in January 1949. A new alignment of young evangelicals was taking place in Wales and was to lead, among other things, to the formation of the Evangelical Movement of Wales. By the mid-1950s Elwyn Davies' time was divided between the leadership of the 'Movement' and IVF student work in the Welsh colleges.

meeting that day, and also have the whole of Tuesday the 26th with you. I merely throw that out as a suggestion. I do not think there will be any difficulty in my being with you at either the end of June or July 1950. We can arrange the exact date later.

Kindly let me know, as soon as you can conveniently, as to whether anything is to happen this next September.

With regard to Caernarvon, I fear I cannot see my way open to being with you at any time this year. Certainly not during the period you mention in November. I am truly sorry, but I know that you will appreciate that I am already more than fully pledged, and that there is a limit to my physical capacity.

With my warmest regards,

Yours very sincerely,

D. M. Lloyd-Jones

Maddeuwch y Saesneg yma. Ond yr wyf fel arfer mewn brys mawr ac nid yw'r un sy'n rhoi help i mi yn deall Cymraeg.

[*Forgive the English. But as usual I am in great haste and the one who helps me does not understand Welsh*]

Books Recommended

39 Mount Park Crescent,
Ealing, London W.5
19 September, 1950

[To Mr E. R. Corsie][1]

Dear Mr Corsie,

The delay in replying to your letter of August 17th is due to the fact that I have been away on holiday.

With regard to the books which I would recommend to you I would suggest the following:– *Systematic Theology* by Charles Hodge, 3 vols. This can only be obtained second hand and it is very difficult even then. On the Word, I recommend *Revelation and Inspiration* by B. B. Warfield, or else *The Infallible Word*. It would also be good for you to obtain the recently re-published *Institutes of the*

---

[1] Future Principal of the Elim Bible College and currently pastor of the Elim Pentecostal Church at St Helens, Merseyside.

Christian Religion by John Calvin, 2 vols. price 30/-. If you master these you really need no more, but of course there are many lesser books which are of great value. I think it would be a good thing for you to write to Dr Douglas Johnson, the InterVarsity Fellowship, 39, Bedford Square, W.C.1 and he may be able to help you to get the Hodge volumes and I believe that they have the other volumes also in stock. Please write to me again if you find trouble in obtaining these books and also let me know if you desire further suggestions at any time. I hope that if you should visit London again you will be good enough to come in to see me. I pray that God may bless you more and more in your ministry and in your personal life.

Yours very sincerely,

D. M. Lloyd-Jones

Counsel for Young Writers

39 Mount Park Crescent
Ealing, London W.5
17 January, 1953

[To Mr O. R. Johnston][1]
Dear Mr Raymond Johnston,

Please forgive me for this delay in acknowledging your very kind letter of the 6th, and in thanking you for your kindness in letting me hear that account of your most interesting conversations at Swanwick. I shall, of course, regard them as confidential. They are

---

[1] O. R. Johnston (1927–85), one of the Oxford graduates responsible for the starting of the Puritan Conference and at this time, with Jim Packer, exercising a new influence in the IVF through the *Christian Graduate* and by other means. From this point onwards ML-J had a new role in counselling wisdom and restraint among young men whose discovery of the Puritans was to cause much excitement. Both by his own ministry, and by prompting James Clarke to republish Calvin's *Institutes* (1949) and J. C. Ryle's *Holiness* (1952), ML-J had been used to prepare the way for this development and critics regarded him as largely responsible for it.

indeed most valuable. The republication of Ryle's 'Holiness' seems to have accomplished even more than I had anticipated.

I feel that Mr Packer and yourself are doing most important work which may well have a great influence in the future. But, you must both learn to 'walk circumspectly'. I mean by this that there is a danger of their dismissing your teaching because of the manner in which it is presented. We must be patient and teach these people in a constructive manner. I write as one who has found it very difficult himself to learn this lesson, but as the years pass I have come to see more and more that the difficulty on the other side is really due to ignorance. We must keep on, and I think we shall find that the really striking change which has already taken place with regard to the views on prophecy will take place also with regard to this other matter.

With regard to the difficulty about explaining the benefits that Keswick and Ruanda seem to give, there are two answers at least.

1. Heresy is often right on many main essentials but goes wrong on just one point. In modern terms this is illustrated often in Pentecostal circles with regard to their doctrine of the Holy Spirit, tongues, healing, etc., while they are absolutely right and orthodox on all essentials and people have real blessing through them

2. The argument from results and benefits is most dangerous. All the cults really thrive on this. I would also query very much whether Keswick really does give a true awareness of sin. I think it is at this point it really fails most of all.

You really must come back to London so that we can talk about these things instead of writing about them.

We all join in kindest regards,

Yours very sincerely,

D. M. Lloyd-Jones

The 'Banner of Truth' Magazine

39 Mount Park Crescent,
Ealing, London W. 5
23 September, 1955

[To Mr Iain H. Murray]
Dear Mr Murray,

I have postponed writing to you until I had had an opportunity of reading a copy of your excellent new magazine[1] I need scarcely say that I think it is excellent, and I have heard similar comments from several others. The only criticism that I have heard is to the effect that the directness of the criticism of modern methods and tendencies may tend to antagonize the very people whom you hope to influence. However, that is a charge that has often been brought against those who are concerned about reform.

I would encourage you, therefore, to continue publishing *The Banner of Truth*, and I pray that God may greatly bless this venture. I am afraid that I have not sufficient knowledge of the technical and business side to be of any help, but if I can be of any help in any small way I shall be very glad and ready to do so.

I hope that you and your wife are well.

With my warmest greetings to you both and also to Mr Norton.

Yours very sincerely,

D. M. Lloyd-Jones

---

[1] The first issue of the *Banner of Truth* magazine had been published at Oxford by the Rev. Sidney Norton and myself. A gift from Westminster Chapel provided half the cost for the second issue.

Have his Views on Sanctification Changed?

39 Mount Park Crescent
Ealing, London W.5
4 February, 1956

[Mr Raymond Johnston]
My dear Friend,

I am truly grateful to you for your most kind letter of the 1st.

The simple answer to your question is that *Christ our Sanctification* still expresses fully what I feel on this question. The confusion arose as a result of a series of sermons I preached on the sealing of the Spirit in Ephesians 1:13. In doing so I said that the interpretation of Acts 19:2, which I gave in the booklet, I would no longer hold, but that it made no difference to what I believed on sanctification, and that in any case that particular interpretation made no difference to the argument of the booklet. The booklet is still on sale in the Bookroom at Westminster Chapel.

I have taken up the matter with Dr D. Johnson and he is going to deal with it. I am truly grateful to you for having drawn my attention to this. I have a feeling that I shall have to publish my five sermons on the Sealing of the Spirit because in one of them I deal at considerable length with the fact that this does not refer directly to sanctification at all.[1]

I should have written to you before this to say that on reflection I am quite sure that your term 'static' with regard to our union with our Lord, in your paper at the Puritan Conference, was absolutely right, and that Mr Kevan's criticism of it was quite wrong. A 'union' of necessity must be static, and the fact that it is static does not mean that it is not vital, or that it is mechanical.

I hope you are both well. We all as a family join in sending our warmest regards to you both.

Yours very sincerely,
D. M. Lloyd-Jones

[1] 'Second blessing' teaching with respect to sanctification was common in the 1950s and hearsay reports of his preaching on Ephesians 1:13 had given rise to the idea that he had changed his view since the material in

'The Major Matter of Policy'

39 Mount Park Crescent,
Ealing, London W.5
31 March, 1956

[To Mr Iain H. Murray]
Dear Mr. Murray,

Many thanks for both your letters. Let me try to deal with them.

The first matter is with regard to dates for meeting Mr Grier. Unfortunately, I have to preach in Wales on May 1st and May 2nd, and shall not be back until the afternoon of Thursday, May 3rd. I observe that Mr. Grier has meetings on the 3rd at 3.30 and 6.30 p.m. That means, I am afraid, that I shall not be able to see him at all, as after my heavy week away I fear I will not be available on Friday the 4th.

I regret this very much but I do not see what can be done. My feeling is that those of you who are available should meet and make your plans.[1]

---

his popular IVF booklet was first published in 1939. It is regrettable that the final proof that his position had not changed was not available until his sermons on Ephesians chapter 1 (preached in 1954–55) were finally published in 1978. See *God's Ultimate Purpose* (Edinburgh: Banner of Truth, 1978), pp. 243–300.

[1] My proposal to ML-J had been for a meeting with the Rev. W. J. Grier (1902–83) of Belfast and the Rev. G. N. M. Collins (1901–89) of Edinburgh, with the intention of arranging a public meeting to launch a new publishing company for the re-issue of reformed and Puritan classics. ML-J's judgment prevailed and no such meeting was arranged. Two months after this letter, however, in May 1956, ML-J invited me to come as his assistant to Westminster Chapel. This led to my friendship with Mr D. J. W. Cullum (1910–71), a young Christian who had recently begun attending services there, and, by his provision, to the formation of the Banner of Truth Trust (July 1957). While ML-J did not become a trustee, and played no direct part, his ministry, under God, had done much to make it possible.

The suggestion about meeting Mr Collins on April 13th is equally impossible for me, as I have to preach at Aberystwyth on April 11th, and shall be travelling back by road on the 12th.

With regard to the major matter of policy, I am not happy with the suggestion of a public meeting. My idea is that we should first publish books and thus create a constituency. If we hurried with a meeting it could only attract a certain type and probably antagonize the very people we want to influence. I feel strongly that the best way is to start very quietly, then to trust God to bless the books that we shall publish. There is all the difference in the world between organizing a movement and the sheer weight of truth producing the movement inevitably. I am simply putting my ideas before you, and I do not in any way want to dampen your ardour.

I wish we could meet together and discuss these things more fully, but I have to leave home for the annual IVF Conference at Swanwick on the 4th as I have said, I shall not be back until April 12th. I wonder if you deem it necessary whether you could come up on Tuesday, April 17th, and we could then meet. We are thinking of you and remembering you these days.

With my warmest regards,

Yours very sincerely,

D. M. Lloyd-Jones

P.S. I assume you will be good enough to let me have all future issues.

Support for a New Centre in North Wales

39 Mount Park Crescent,
Ealing, London W.5
28 April, 1958

[To the Rev. Elwyn Davies][1]

My Dear Friend,

I am just writing a word with the enclosed cheque from Dr Joseph Evans. He had, as you will remember, promised to send me this but it only arrived last week. Actually I have seen him since

---

[1] In March 1958 the growing Evangelical Movement of Wales had

then and he was down here spending Saturday evening with us. I am sure that he is going to do something really substantial for us, for he kept returning to it. From what he said it may take a little time to deal with certain matters before he will be in a position to give us the help, but I am certain that it is coming, and we must therefore keep on praying hopefully and with confidence. He was greatly impressed with the possibilities of Eryl Aran. Will you please write to him and thank him for this gift? I assume that you have already done so in the case of Mr John Laing.

What is the position with regard to the Income Tax authorities? Kindly let me know when that matter is put right, so that I can act. You will also let Mr D. J. James's Trustees know so that they can act also.

Maddeuwch y gair yma yn Saesneg, ond mae braidd yn gyfyng arnaf. Cofion annwyl atoch i gyd,

[*Forgive this word in English but I am rather hard-pressed. Warmest greetings to you all*]

    D. M. Lloyd-Jones

---

purchased for £7,000 a very suitable property, 'Eryl Aran', on the shore of Bala lake, for the use of staff, for offices and for camps and conferences. At the time of purchase the Movement, after paying the deposit, had only enough funds left to pay the wages bill for one month. ML-J was scarcely in his element as a fund-raiser but when he believed something had major spiritual importance he did not hesitate. In 1960 the Movement acquired the more advantageous adjoining property, 'Bryn-y-groes', to which the work at Eryl Aran was transferred. This became and remains a key centre for camps and conferences.

Dr Joseph Evans was a native of North Wales who had emigrated to the United States. During the revival of 1904 he had come under conviction of sin and fled to work in the mines of Troedyrhiw, South Wales. It is said that he was converted in one of Evan Roberts' meetings.

The Start of the 'Evangelical Magazine'

39 Mount Park Crescent
Ealing, London W.5
5 May, 1958

[To the Rev. Elwyn Davies]
My dear Friend,

Please forgive me for my forgetfulness in not sending the enclosed cheque when I wrote to you last week. I fear that in the excitement of the birthday and my being in Scotland the previous week-end I forgot all about it. This is to cover the expenses of Mr Caswell from N. Ireland, and also a contribution either to you personally in the matter of providing hospitality for us all, or to the Movement.[1]

Elizabeth Braund came to see me yesterday about the question of the magazine. I had to tell her that I really cannot take an active part in this. I am already doing far too much, and I cannot undertake any further responsibilities which would involve me in regular attendance at Committees or any detail work. I told her that I felt therefore that I must withdraw from the Committee. I shall, of course, still be interested and ready to help in any consultative manner.

It seems to me that you and Elizabeth Braund and Packer should meet fairly soon in order to plan the first issue. It is very important that this should be done properly.

Maddeuwch y gair yma yn Saesneg ac mewn brys mawr.

[*Forgive this word in English and in great haste*]

Warmest greetings,

D. M. Lloyd-Jones

---

[1] At a meeting in Bala in April, attended by a small group of leaders, including Dr R. N. Caswell, Principal of the Belfast Bible College, plans were laid for a new *Evangelical Magazine*. The already instituted *Evangelical Magazine of Wales* was largely to join forces, but plans for Irish and Scots participation did not materialise. Elizabeth Braund, chief editor of the new magazine, had been converted in connection with the ministry at Westminster Chapel in the early 1950s.

A Busy Summer

39 Mount Park Crescent
Ealing, London W.5
2 June, 1958

[To the Rev. Elwyn Davies]
My dear Friend

I have just written a word to Elizabeth Braund to confirm Wednesday June 11th. I have suggested that 2 p.m. at the Chapel might be suitable for us. If you would prefer it later, please let me know. I am free until about 5.30 p.m.

I fear I must also let you know now that I cannot be at the Ministers' gatherings at Cilgwyn. I am having an exceptionally busy time. I am, as you know, going to South Africa and now I have had an additional task thrust upon me by the Christian Medical Fellowship of preparing some kind of a statement on the Wolfenden Report. I felt I had to do this as for some reason there does not seem to be anybody else who could do it. As I was not due to speak at Cilgwyn I feel I am not in any way letting you down, and you understand the position. I can explain more fully when we meet.

Gwn y deallwch sut y mae arnaf ac y credwch fi pan y dywedaf ei bod yn wir ddrwg gennyf nad allaf fod yng Nghilgwyn.

Cofion annwyl fel arfer,

[*I know you will understand how it is with me and that you will believe me when I say that I am very sorry that I cannot be at Cilgwyn*]

Warmest regards as always,
D. M. Lloyd-Jones

P.S. Os ydych am drafod pethau yng Nghymru gennyf rhowch wybod. Byddaf oddi cartref fory a dydd Mercher ond byddaf gartref nos Iau, Gwener a Sadwrn os bydd eisiau ffonio arnoch.
[*If you wish to discuss things in Wales with me, let me know. I shall be away from home tomorrow and on Wednesday but I shall be home Thursday night, Friday and Saturday, if you need to phone*]

'Better Times are Coming'

39 Mount Park Crescent,
Ealing, London W.5
11 January, 1961

[To Mr Peter Golding]¹
My Dear Peter,

. I feel I must write to thank you for your exceptionally kind and good letter. I have rarely received a letter that has given me so much joy and encouragement.

It was very good of you to take the trouble to write it.

It is a matter of constant regret that owing to the ridiculously busy life that I have to live that I do not see more of you in private. Please do not hesitate to come to see me whenever you would like to do so.

I am particularly impressed by the understanding – intellectual and spiritual which you show.

You are quite right that I am primarily an evangelist. It is a measure of the terrible spiritual aberration of these days that that is not recognised.

May God continue to bless you and to manifest Himself to you. Do not be discouraged. Better times are coming. Let us stand together and work and pray until 'the glorious morning dawns'.

With my warmest regards,

Yours very sincerely,

D. M. Lloyd-Jones

¹ One of a number of students for the ministry belonging to Westminster Chapel. ML-J preached at Mr Golding's induction at Hayes Town Chapel, Middlesex, in 1966.

7

ON EVANGELICAL UNITY AND THE THREAT OF ECUMENISM

A Wider Unity in England?

Rosapenna Hotel,
County Donegal
30 August, 1955

[Mr and Mrs H. F. R. Catherwood][1]
My Dear Fred and Elizabeth,

Many thanks for your letter and the enclosed statement on 'The Future of the Assemblies'. I think the latter is excellent in every way, the statement is clear and as an introduction of the subject I cannot imagine anything better.

I am writing in a hurry in order that you may have these few ideas of mine as soon as possible.

With regard to your question concerning persons, my feeling is that you have put it generally in terms of opinion and that therefore it is not too strong. Actually my feeling is this, that the number of those who are prepared to *do* anything by way of giving a lead is very small. On the other hand I am convinced that if something along these lines became an accomplished fact and

---

[1] Elizabeth, their elder daughter, had married Fred Catherwood the previous year. Having joined Westminster Chapel from a Brethren background, Mr Catherwood had a close interest in discussions on changes which were then going on among the Brethren, and upon the possibilities which these changes presented for a larger unity among evangelical churches in England. This was a subject of major concern for ML-J who, as early as 1947, had proposed to the members of Westminster Chapel a withdrawal from the Congregational Union on account of its liberalism. See *D. Martyn Lloyd-Jones: The Fight of Faith*, p. 164.

large numbers of assemblies were ready to call ministers,[1] then many ministers would jump at the opportunity and leave the denominations to which they now belong. It is at that point that courage will be demanded of the few who must act as leaders and pioneers. As regards Kevan and D.J. I fear that, owing to their positions, they must be included among the many rather than the few. They are sympathetic and would be ready to follow rather than to lead.

The only points in your statement which I feel need to be elaborated and explained in conversation are the following:

Page 8, para 4 in section x. I feel that the reference to 'one body' at the end of the first sentence is likely to frighten people as it suggests a new denomination with central control. What we visualise surely is a free 'association' or 'fellowship' of local independent churches which are quite autonomous. They will cooperate with each other and help each other, support the same college (LBC),[2] same missionary societies etc. But the LBC would not be their college etc., etc.

Page 10, Section xii. Para 1. This is too loose and would lead to chaos. There must be some kind of definition here and general conformity to a pattern.

The assemblies would concede the need of a one-man ministry for instance. The others would accept a 'breaking of bread' meeting, but not as the regular and only Sunday morning service but as an additional service held either before or after the service for preaching and exposition. Attendance at the breaking of bread service every Sunday would not be obligatory but a minimum number of attendances per annum could be agreed upon.

As regards baptism, I believe agreement could be obtained along the following lines – no baptism of infants; mode of baptism to be

[1] At this date dissatisfaction with a plurality of teachers in the assemblies was creating interest in the need for ministers. Within twenty years this trend was to undergo a major reverse at the hands of the charismatic movement and the 'one man ministry' became cried down in the evangelical churches generally.

[2] The London Bible College. ML-J had been a principal supporter of the College and it also had Brethren backers.

left to individual preference. But even here I would be prepared to negotiate. However, to leave it quite open would I fear lead to contention and endless arguments and disputations, the real difficulty being infants.[1]

Apart from that I really have nothing to add. Your statement is thoroughly balanced and comprehensive apart from the above two points. And you even cover them by saying that you are really only laying down general principles for discussion. Your general case is, I feel, masterly and unanswerable. Excellent!

Fondest love to you both,
     Your ever loving Father

Controversy with Aneirin Talfan Davies on Christian Unity

Ealing,
London W.5
April, 1963

[To the Editor of *Barn*][2]
Sir,

Before I ask you for some of your space in order to answer some of the comments of my old friend Aneirin Talfan Davies[3] in [his column] *Ar Ymyl y Ddalen* [In the Margin] in your March issue,

---

[1] Unlike some other parts of the British Isles, strong evangelical churches practising infant baptism were practically extinct in England at this date. It was this fact, rather than any wish to exclude paedo-baptist churches from a wider unity, which explains his words. A chief reason why he pressed for unity through the British Evangelical Council rather than through the Fellowship of Independent Evangelical Churches in the 1960s was that the former could include paedo-baptist and Presbyterian congregations.

[2] *Barn* (lit. 'Opinion'), April 1963 (Llyfrau'r Dryw: Llandybie and Swansea), pp. 171–3. ML-J's letter is here translated by Dafydd Ifans from his original which was in Welsh.

[3] Aneirin Talfan Davies (1909–80), son of a Calvinistic Methodist minister who became a critic, poet and broadcaster. He had interviewed ML-J on Welsh television in a series of programmes entitled 'Dylanwadau' (Influences) in March 1962 and was second editor to *Barn*, a monthly magazine also founded in that year.

let me congratulate you on your excellent monthly periodical. I gain great pleasure from reading it and I firmly believe that it will do much good.

I am grateful to Mr Talfan Davies for his kind spirit, and I believe, as he says, that he did not wish to do me wrong, although he says at the same time that I consider myself as being infallible and am as self-righteous as the Pharisees of old. I am not surprised that my friend admits that he is in 'a great quandary'. I shall attempt to show him what accounts for this, although it is difficult to do so in a letter such as this. I shall take his points according to their order in his article:

The IVF and the SCM
This is the old complaint – the IVF's refusal to co-operate with the SCM in the Colleges. To ATD [Aneirin Talfan Davies] this is intolerable. But before we judge, we should ask first of all, what accounts for this attitude? The answer is this, that it is based on the same principle that forces the Bishop of St. David's not to allow his priests to officiate together with ministers of other denominations, and that causes the Anglicans to refuse to sit together with their fellow-Christians at the Lord's table in Communion even at ecumenical conferences.

It is not wise for those who live in glass houses to throw stones! After all, there is such a thing as consistency, and there must be some relation between belief and principles and behaviour. Of course, if we no longer believe in principles, and if we are nothing better than utilitarians, then we have no difficulty at all. But with some of us (the Pharisees again, supposedly!) honesty of the mind still counts, and we cannot renounce in our deeds that which we believe in our hearts. We must have agreement on basic points before true co-operation is possible. That is the main thrust of my argument in my booklet.[1]

If ATD does not agree with this, then he had better enquire a

---

[1] *The Basis Of Christian Unity: An Exposition of John 17 and Ephesians 4* (London: IVF, 1962), repr. in *Knowing the Times* (Edinburgh: Banner of Truth, 1989).

little of his bishops and of his archbishop especially, but let him be careful lest he should be dominated by a sort of nonconformist 'hangover'![1]

Church Unity

ATD claims that I do not believe in church unity. But on what basis? The title of the booklet which he attacks is proof and sufficient answer in itself – *The Basis of Christian Unity*. It presupposes, does it not, that I believe that the church should be one. And I say that perfectly clearly in my introduction, and more than that, that I look upon schism as sin.

But it is one thing to believe in church unity, it is another thing to believe in the present ecumenical movement. That is why I stress the importance of the foundations. Before we rush to 'do something' unthinkingly and in a state of panic, we must first of all face questions such as: What is a Christian? What is the church? What is the nature of true unity? 'Can two walk together, except they be agreed?'.

If it is of interest, my belief is that all the denominations in Wales (including the Episcopal Church) should join together at once as there is nothing of any importance theologically or doctrinally which separates them! But, to follow the same principle exactly, it cannot be expected of those who disagree with them, on essential and basic questions, that they should be part of that united church. (I show in my booklet what the basic criteria are).

Authority

ATD sees this as being all-important. He says: 'There is only one authority – the Bible'. But it is not at all clear whether this is the opinion of ATD himself, or whether he is merely quoting my position. That is my belief, but I am not clear whether ATD agrees with me. Is tradition equal in authority with the Bible in his opinion? Is he on the threshold of Roman Catholicism? To

[1] A humorous reference to the fact that by this date ATD had moved from Calvinistic Methodism to the Church in Wales which ML-J refers to below as the 'Episcopal Church'.

the Protestant, the Bible is the only authority on all matters of faith and life. But how are we to interpret the Bible? ATD is frightened by the idea that the individual has any right in this matter at all. And at this point his standpoint is in fact laughable. On what grounds did he leave the Calvinistic Methodists – the denomination of his fathers – and decide to become a member of the Episcopal Church? (By the way, he was, by doing that, condemning everyone else who stayed with the Methodists). The answer is, of course, that he came to that decision by using his reason and his understanding. Let us respect him for thinking for himself and for acting according to his convictions. After all, the individual who decides to subject his mind and his reason to the Pope and to the Church of Rome, decides to do that for himself! He alone is the authority at that all-important moment.

But what is the final authority in this matter? Is it the bishops? Or is it the Pope and the Church of Rome, or the Councils of the early church? Let us allow the twenty-first article of the articles of the Church of England to answer the question:

> 'General Councils may not be gathered together without the commandment and will of Princes. And when they be gathered together, (forasmuch as they be an assembly of men, whereof all be not governed with the Spirit and Word of God) they may err, and sometimes have erred, even in things pertaining unto God. Wherefore things ordained by them as necessary to salvation have neither strength nor authority, unless it may be declared that they be taken out of holy Scripture.'

We know that nearly all the bishops erred with Arius in the fourth century, and that the situation was saved by an individual – *Athanasius contra mundum*. But to ATD that sort of thing was 'arrogance'. What do we say also of Luther standing by himself against all the authorities of the church and the traditions of centuries – 'Here I stand. I can do no other. So help me God' – and many like him over the centuries? This is the essence of

Protestantism. But more important than all these considerations is the question, What of the teaching of the New Testament? see 1 John 2:20, 'But ye have an unction from the Holy One, and ye know all things'.

This does not mean 'total freedom' at all. Indeed every man who is led of the Holy Ghost is a modest man. He knows of his own failings and weaknesses and he is aware of his ignorance daily. Consequently he enquires of others through reading and talking to them and he will respect their understanding in the Scriptures. ATD says – if man is to use his own mind and reason – 'What is the point, therefore, in speaking of a church at all?' The simple answer is that a church is composed of saints who are gathered together, i.e. people who agree with each other to worship God, and to assist each other in the light and under the leadership of the Holy Spirit, and under the lordship of the Lord Jesus Christ who promised to be present with them. The truth is that these 'Catholics' do not believe at all in the 'unity of the Spirit'. The only unity they know of is the unity of bishops – 'episcopal bureaucracy' according to P. T. Forsyth.

As ATD has mentioned the point, I may as well say that I still believe the Calvinistic Methodist Confession of Faith. The point which grieves me most is that the majority of the Calvinistic Methodists in Wales today do not believe it any more, and they do not even see the need for a confession of faith at all. I also believe wholeheartedly everything which is contained in the church covenant of Westminster Chapel (the belief of the Independent Protestant Dissenters). I would not be able to stay there as minister for a moment if this were not true, although ATD does not believe this! I am surprised at ATD's inconsistency. On the one hand, he attacks the IVF and myself for having a 'Basis of Faith', and because we stick to it, and because we decide membership of the societies by that basis. On the other hand, he condemns us at the same time for being some sort of spiritual anarchists, everyone for himself, without thinking about anyone else!

What is there to account for this mix-up in his mind? The explanation is clear enough.

The Visible and Invisible Church

I begin with the personal side because I am accused – 'but Dr Lloyd-Jones does not believe in a visible Church'. This is surprising! How can a man be a church member at all, let alone be a minister of a church, if he does not believe in a visible church? But more than that, as I have said already, the title of my booklet is: *The Basis of Christian Unity*! To prove the point ATD quotes from my booklet:

> 'The invisible church is more important than the visible church, and loyalty to the former may involve either expulsion or separation from the latter, and the formation of a *new* visible church'.[1]

Then ATD goes on to say: 'Notice the word which I have italicised (*new*), because this is the heart of the argument'. Yes, indeed, this is the heart of the argument, because it shows in a very clear way the surprising 'myopia' which is a feature of the followers of the Catholic teaching. When ATD saw the word *new*, like a true Catholic, he lost his head and reason, and he became blind to everything else. A new church! A church other than the Episcopal Church! Impossible! 'The word "new" must be italicised here!' He does not see anything in the sentence apart from the word 'new' – and yet the reader will see that the word which follows the word 'new' is '*visible* church'!

But, to be more serious, the stumbling block to ATD is that I differentiate between the visible church and the invisible church. I find it difficult to believe this of one who has interested himself so much in church matters, but I get the impression that ATD is under the impression that I am saying something new by emphasizing this difference, and that I appear as a sort of authoritative pope announcing some new heresy. I believe, rather, that he dislikes the idea, and it is his dislike of the idea that causes him to write such irresponsible things.

Does he not know that every Protestant church (in contrast to the Roman Catholic Church) emphasizes the importance of

[1] See *Knowing the Times*, p.160.

this difference? The point is all-important in these present days, when so many Protestants are ready to return to Rome.

Let me prove what I say by Article xix of the Church of England:

> 'The visible church of Christ is a congregation of faithful men, in the which the pure Word of God is preached . . . As the Church of Jerusalem, Alexandria, and Antiochia, have erred; so also the Church of Rome hath erred, not only in their living and manner of Ceremonies, but also in matters of Faith'.

Notice the word 'visible'. Every authority on the Articles agrees that it suggests a contrast with the 'invisible' church. Let us listen to Richard Hooker (not 'one of these hotheaded evangelicals' but 'the judicious Hooker'):

> 'That Church of Christ, which we properly term His body mystical, can be but one; neither can that one be sensibly discerned by any man, inasmuch as the parts thereof are some in heaven already with Christ, and the rest that are on earth (albeit, their natural persons be visible) we do not discern under this property whereby they are truly and infallibly of that body . . . For lack of diligent observing the difference between the Church of God mystical and visible, the oversights are neither few nor light that have been committed' (*Eccl. Pol.* Bk. iii, pp. 2, 9).

For a change, I have an urge to italicise, especially the last sentence!

Archbishop Benson agrees when he speaks, in his introduction to his book on Cyprian, of 'the noble, and alas, too fruitful error of arraying the visible church in the attributes of the church invisible'.

But Dr W. H. Griffith Thomas in his standard book – *The Principles of Theology: An Introduction to the Thirty-Nine Articles* – is clearer still. He says this:

> 'No one questions the fact of visibility. The only question is as to any precise form of visibility being of the *esse* . . . All attempts to identify the visible with the invisible will only lead to

confusion and trouble, as in the past . . . The true Church, or Body of Christ, is thus invisible by reason of the vital union of its individual members with Christ, which is of necessity invisible . . . In the true Christian [Dr Griffith Thomas did not belong to the IVF] both aspects are joined, but in the mere professing Christian they are not, so that the Body of Christ is neither separate from nor identical with the sum total of visible Churches.

'The difference of visibility and invisibility turns on the relative importance in which these two aspects are regarded. If, following the Church of Rome, visibility is made the primary antecedent, one result will follow. If, in harmony with the New Testament, visibility is made the consequent of spiritual life within, another and very different consequence will ensue. Rome makes this visibility to be of the essence of the Church, while Anglicanism, following the New Testament, makes invisible or spiritual union with Christ the vital and fundamental requirement. Even allowing that the terms "visible" and "invisible" represent controversial conditions of the sixteenth century, the truth expressed by them is valid, because the distinction is between a real and an apparent Church, between spiritual reality and outward manifestations. The point of the term "visible" is that the reality is not identical with, or simply expressed by, the outward manifestations. The New Testament idea of the Church is never indifferent to visibility or order, but it nevertheless puts the main stress on spiritual gift and grace and not on institutions and organisations'.[1]

These are the words of a man who was the Principal of Wycliffe College, Oxford, a member of the Church of England. It is obvious that ATD does not follow either the New Testament or the teaching of the Church of England! The truth is that he is in a dreadful quandary which forces him to contradict himself. At one moment the poet and the literary figure looms large and

---

[1] W. H. Griffith Thomas, *The Principles of Theology: An Introduction to the Thirty-Nine Articles* (London: Longmans, Green and Co., 1930), pp. 270–71.

he quotes from the translation by John Thomas of Rhayader of Isaac Watts' wonderful words: 'The Church of God through heaven and earth is one ...' Then the churchman and the Catholic get a grip on him again and he declares clearly: 'If there is something which is undeniably plain in the Bible, then that is, that the church is a visible society'. Is the church in heaven visible? No! Isaac Watts' theology was a lot clearer than that of ATD and it allowed him to perceive the difference between the invisible church and the visible church. My claim is the claim of those authorities which I quoted – every one of them an Anglican. This is why I say, in the words which were quoted by ATD: 'We must never *start* with the visible church, or an institution, but rather with the truth which alone creates unity'.

Oh! that I had not italicised the word *start*! Then ATD would not have misunderstood the thrust of the booklet or gone on to condemn those who say that the religion of Jesus Christ is a 'spiritual religion'. What sort of religion is it then?

The root of all his error is his belief in the Catholic doctrine which teaches 'The Theology of Incarnation', namely that the church is an extension of the Incarnation. The emphasis is wholly on the visible, consequently the invisible is ignored, and sometimes, sad to say, it is even ridiculed – as the same people often also ridicule any emphasis on the experience of salvation and conversion.

This failure to see the place of the individual within the life of the church, the tendency to emphasize tradition and to make it co-equal with the authority of the Bible, and all of it in the end based on the idea of apostolic succession, leads to two very serious results. I can best set them out by quoting the words of two famous theologians. P. T. Forsyth in his *Christ and the Sacraments* says:

'The Apostolic succession was at first a succession of truth rather than of persons, till in time the depositories became more than the deposit. The Church fell into a bureaucracy in the sense that the officers vouched for the matter more than the matter for the officers'.

Principal John Huxtable in his preface to *The True Nature of a Gospel Church* by John Owen, adds:

'When Anglicans talk of the Church they almost always give the impression of meaning the hierarchy and the priesthood, almost as if the laity were little more than a necessary background to the labours of bishop, priest and deacon'.

He also says:

'A Congregational minister and his people are so closely knit that he cannot function without them; and this is an indication of the belief that Church acts are indeed acts of the Church and not simply of Church officials'.[1]

The truth is that there is very little similarity between the New Testament church and a cathedral, or in fact a parish church. If one is to see a true church one must attend a prayer meeting, or an experience meeting, or a fellowship. In spite of all the confusion, I fear that I must admit that many a Pentecostal church is more similar to some of the churches of the New Testament than our churches, with their conceited dignity, their dead formality and their respectability, their dress and processions and their ceremonies – which remind someone more of the Old Testament rather than the New, and of the temples of the pagan false religions rather than the simplicity of the Early Church with her meetings in private homes.

Split Chapels[2]
ATD always comes back to the question of the individual. It is obvious that he hates people such as Savonarola and Luther, Calvin, John Knox and John Penry; Puritans such as Walter Cradoc and Vavasor Powell and others, as well as Methodists like Howell Harris

---

[1] *The True Nature of a Gospel Church* (James Clarke: London, 1947), p. 15.

[2] The Welsh original, *'capeli split'*, contains more meaning than any one corresponding phrase in English. The idea is of congregations going their own way and then splitting in half over doctrinal differences or for reasons less doctrinal, i.e., personalities.

and Daniel Rowland, George Whitefield and John Wesley. The reason for that is that these people dared to stand against bishops and church authorities and tradition. Poor old John Penry – that hot-headed individual who was so sure of his opinion and of his belief that he refused to bend the knee to the bishops, or to Queen Elizabeth I.

It would appear also from ATD's article that these evangelical individuals do not touch real life at all. It is obvious that Catholicism paralyses the memory also! No one paid more attention to personal inner experience than Oliver Cromwell and his co-Puritans. Who would dare to bring this accusation against Howell Harris, founder of 'The Agricultural Society of Breconshire'? And what about William Wilberforce and Shaftesbury? The personal and intimate experience of Christ is the key to the activities of all these people. Indeed, it would not be difficult to show that it is these people who have *done* things over the centuries and that in spite of the opposition and persecution of church authorities and traditions.

There is no space to deal with ATD's remarks about the apostle Paul. But in my booklet I have tried to explain in detail his teaching on the question of unity in Ephesians 4:1–16. No one was more intolerant of false doctrine than the great apostle. Love, meekness and patience towards the ones who stumbled on life's paths, but severity towards false apostles and deceivers! We may be quite certain too that no one would have had any hope of being a church member in Paul's day without knowing what he believed and without experience of 'salvation and conversion'. The church was, in the apostle's days, 'an élite clique' of the saved (ATD's words). Oh! that we might be able to return to this same idea instead of insulting it!

I have not the least shame in owning the idea of 'a split chapel'. What was the Early Church to the Sadducees and Pharisees but a 'split chapel'? What is the Anglican Church to the Catholics? A 'split chapel'! What were the Puritan churches (Congregational and Baptist) to the Anglicans? A 'split chapel'! What were the Calvinist and Wesleyan Methodists to the Church authorities? 'Split chapels'! It is an honour to be a descendant of such a lineage and to belong to such a company.

I am sorry that my dear friend has wandered so far as to be able to speak as he does about his spiritual pedigree and heritage.

I am surprised at him as a Christian but just as much as a Welshman. If he had, like Mr Saunders Lewis[1] turned Catholic, I would understand and would see a kind of consistency, although of course I would disagree completely. The essence of Anglicanism, however, is the English way of thinking which rejects reason and definitions and is anti-theological, and that likes to think of itself in terms of 'empiricism', 'comprehension', 'uniformity' and the *'via media'*.

How different from the Protestants on the Continent in the 16th century! How different from the Scots, yes, how different from the Welshman's nature. The Welshman, because he is unusually intelligent and is a man of strong principles, is nearly always in difficulties with the English. The Englishman looks upon him as a rebel, as an awkward individualist, as a man who always wants his own way and is perpetually creating totally uncalled for difficulties.

The Welshman is not a 'party man' and he cannot come to terms with the idea of the 'Establishment'. That is his story ever since he stopped being Papist. This is true of him in his religion and in his politics. The Englishman cannot understand why the Welshman speaks so much about his country, his nation, his nature, his culture and his language. 'Why don't the Welsh forget these unimportant things', he says, 'and why doesn't he conform with us and with everyone else?'

But here we have ATD of all people, using such phrases as that, and saying that to be different, to think for one's self, and to refuse to conform with the majority because you believe in principles, is the great sin!

I venture to prophesy that the great battle of the future in Wales will be the battle between the Roman Catholics and the despised

---

[1] Saunders Lewis (1893–1985), a leading Welsh dramatist, scholar and literary figure and Welsh Nationalist, son of a Presbyterian minister, who became a Roman Catholic.

Evangelical people – the only two groups which know where they stand and what they believe. The first question and the all-important one today is, not how we are to unite the denominations as they stand, but the old 16th century question – how is man saved? Is it through the church and its sacraments and through works alone; or is it justification by faith alone?

I am not without hope that some day we shall see ATD 'coming to his senses' in the midst of the spiritual famine of the *ecclesia anglicana*. When that happens, he too will realise as, mercifully, Mr D. Gwenallt Jones has already done,[1] that he has not embraced the 'Old Mother', but as Gwenallt says, 'the Old Traitoress'.

Yours faithfully,
D. Martyn Lloyd-Jones

Aneirin Talfan Davies' Response[2]

ATD accused ML-J of avoiding the issue of the divisive attitude of IVF members in colleges and believed that his references to the Bishop of St. David's, and the question of communion, were red herrings. He regarded ML-J's professed concern for Christian unity as unpardonable cynicism. The minister of Westminster Chapel obviously had no time for anyone who could not follow the blinkered fundamentalism which rapes man's intellect and breeds self-righteousness of the worst kind. He discussed ML-J's speculation as to ATD's reason for leaving the Calvinistic Method-ists. ATD felt called to leave the denomination and had no quarrel with anyone who felt obliged to stay within it. He retained friend-ship with the two ministers who cared for him while he was in the

---

[1] Gwenallt Jones (1899–1969), a Christian poet who moved from Nonconformity, via the social gospel, to Anglicanism before returning to Calvinistic Methodism.

[2] I give this short précis of the response published by ATD in the May 1963 issue of *Barn* so that the reader can better understand ML-J's second letter.

denomination and never tried to proselytise anyone from his previous denomination or from any other denomination.

ATD returned to the question of the authority of Scripture and believed that ML-J should have quoted Article xx ('Of the Authority of the Church') which ATD accepted, and which he supported with a quotation from Richard Hooker. As an Anglican, ATD did not accept the Roman Catholic teaching of the Council of Trent which placed tradition side by side with Scripture but he argued that men, no doubt under the influence of the Holy Spirit, were responsible for laying down the canon of Scripture. So the church should have the authority to explain Scripture. His conclusion was that ML-J had either gone a long way towards classical Nonconformity or that he was merely playing with words.

ATD criticised ML-J for omitting a reference to the sacraments in his use of Article xix. He believed that the sacraments brought the church into unity with Christ and the invisible church. The church is the body of Christ and because that is so, any rents or divisions within her are sinful and Christ is recrucified. He was willing for ML-J to criticise him as a Christian (no-one is above reproach) but not to doubt him as a Welshman. For years, he claimed, ML-J had been ministering to contented middle-class sheep in the centre of the English capital – among the English whom he so much despised. If ATD had chosen to become a Roman Catholic, he would have received praise from ML-J. He could understand the attraction of Rome for ML-J, it was all part of a love-hate complex which did not allow him to leave that Church alone. ML-J could not think of the future in Wales except as a great battle between Roman Catholics and Evangelicals. It was no wonder he returned to the sixteenth century and persisted with the old battles in terms which have long since lost their force.

ATD did not hate Luther, or Calvin, or Penry, or Walter Cradoc, and as for Howell Harris, ATD belonged to the same Church as he did.

Controversy Continued

Ealing,
London W.5
June, 1963

[To the Editor of *Barn*][1]
Sir,

Once again I ask you for some space to answer the comments of my friend Mr Aneirin Talfan Davies [ATD]. I thank him for his answer to my previous letter. I shall try to limit myself to the original matters which he raised.

Causes of Concern

I fear that the tendency to misunderstand, to read implications into what was said, and to doubt and to be suspicious of other people's motives, were as present in the second article as they were in the first. For example:

1.   ATD says that for me to say that I believe the denominations should unite together and that the evangelicals should come together is just a load of cynicism. Why cynicism? The fact is that I believe from the bottom of my heart in church unity and I look on schism as sin. That which I attempted to emphasise in my booklet *The Basis of Christian Unity* is the foundation of that unity. I think it sinful for religious people who are agreed on the essential points to stay apart only because of tradition. And I emphasise the phrase 'the essential points'. I mean doctrines such as the Being of God, the Deity of Christ, the Incarnation, the miracles, the propitiatory death, the resurrection of Christ (literally in the body), his ascension, the person of the Holy Spirit, justification through faith and regeneration, and not some 'mint and anise', as, for example, what sort of wine one should use for the sacrament of the Lord's supper.

2.   I am afraid also that ATD has misunderstood completely what I said about Welshness and the English way of thinking. He says

[1] June 1963, pp. 236–7.

that I reproach him for not being a true Welshman, and he goes on to say that I despise the English. What I did was state my surprise that a Welshman such as 'ATD of all people' had fallen into this trap. And it was not English people that I had in mind either but 'the English way of thinking'. ATD must start to think in terms of principles and ideas, without personalising them perpetually. To me, as I attempted to show, the English way of thinking is dangerous to true Protestantism. I believe the same of the Greek way of thinking as compared with the Hebrew way of thinking. But that does not mean that I despise the Greeks! I hope that I do not despise any person, but I admit to despising social or intellectual snobbery, and especially in the religious realm. I feel a true compassion for the person who scornfully rejects the evangelical faith, and I have proved that to be so, I believe, by spending the greater part of my life trying to convince them. In the same way as ATD has remained friendly with his former ministers, I also have friends among them, and I am always ready to have dealings with them. I strongly believe that some of them are wrong, and I say so strongly, not to scorn them, but to try to lead them to the truth. I shall let your readers judge between us on this matter of despising and scorn, but they must re-read ATD's first article in addition to his reply.

Satisfaction

I rejoice that ATD's answer has cleared up two of the important points which he raised:

1.   The Visible and Invisible Church: As ATD agrees that the church is invisible as well as being visible, and is ready to admit that his statement in the first article was open-ended when he said (while criticising my emphasis on the invisible side, and drawing the erroneous conclusion that I did not believe in a visible church): 'If one thing is totally clear in the Bible, then that is that the church is a visible society' – there is no need to say any more. All is well!

2.   The Individual: The main point of his attack upon the members of the IVF was that the individual was his own authority,

and that he functioned in that way. I answered by saying that ATD himself was acting in the same way exactly by joining the Episcopal Church. And my friend now agrees and says: 'By leaving the Calvinistic Methodists, I did nothing more than follow my conviction . . . all I can say is that that was *my* call' (ATD's own emphasis). Splendid! Yes, *my* call, to me the individual. But why is it then that he refuses the same right to those individuals who wish to follow their convictions by joining the IVF, and who are convinced that they cannot co-operate with a movement such as the SCM, a movement which has shown clearly to the world what it is in fact by publishing the well-publicised book by the Bishop of Woolwich – *Honest to God*? If it is in order for ATD to follow his convictions and to do the proper thing in his own mind, why does he fling such scorn and sarcasm at those who carry out exactly the same principle? Yes, these are matters for the individual in the first case. But let us turn to other facets of ATD's difficulties in this context.

The Point of View of the IVF

I should just like to add a short word to Mr D. Ioan Davies' excellent letter in your current issue. The members of the IVF act exactly as the Methodist fathers did. They remain members of their own churches, and they are encouraged to do so. But for the purpose of evangelistic work in the colleges, and of nurturing their faith in the face of considerable hostility in their colleges at this time, they form societies similar to the Methodist societies. Naturally, they have their own rules, and they look upon their societies not as some form of forum to argue about the foundations of faith, but as an opportunity for those who already agree with each other to associate and to bear witness. The one great difference between them and the Methodist societies is that they are not so scrupulous and exacting in their discipline as the Methodists. And by the way, it was not because they believed that the Anglican Church held the true light that the Methodist fathers remained within her, but because they saw her piteous state and her terrible darkness, and because they knew that they would lose the chance to reform her if they were to leave. (See especially *The Early Years of Methodism* by Richard Bennett).[1]

Authority

But, after all, the major problem is the problem of authority, and especially in relation to explaining and interpreting the Bible.

ATD's trap is 'tradition', as it is also to all who hold Catholic ideas. Sometimes he makes clear statements such as, for example, when he says that tradition is not co-equal with the Scriptures – and let us be thankful for that. On the other hand, he is enticed by the notion of tradition to such an extent that he is guilty of contradicting totally, in the most lucid way, what the Apostle Paul teaches. After quoting the first verses of 1 Corinthians 15 and italicising the words 'which I also received' – he goes on to say – 'St. Paul received the tradition from the hands of men, and he transmitted it faithfully to his audience'. But is this true? From whom did the apostle receive his message? It is an all-important question and fortunately we were not left in any uncertainty concerning it. This is not a matter of opinion. The apostle himself answers the question as follows: 'For I have received of the *Lord* that which also I delivered unto you . . .' (1 Cor. 11:23); '. . . If ye have heard of the dispensation of the grace of God which is given me to you-ward: *How that by revelation he made known unto me the mystery* . . .' (Eph. 3:2–3): But clearer still, and as if they were written specifically to answer ATD's error, : 'But I certify you, brethren, that the gospel which was preached of me is not after man. For I neither received it of man, neither was I taught it, *but by the revelation of Jesus Christ*' (Gal. 1:11–12). What could be clearer? ATD says, 'St. Paul received the tradition from the hands of men'. St. Paul says, 'For I neither received it of man, neither was I taught it'.

The truth is, of course, that that which made Paul an apostle and gave him apostolic authority, was the fact that he had seen the risen Jesus, and had accepted his message from him personally. Paul did not receive it through the tradition of the church; he was, rather,

[1] Caernarvon, 1909; repr. Banner of Truth, 1962, and Evangelical Movement of Wales, 1987.

with the other apostles and prophets, part of the foundation on which the church was built (Eph. 2:20).

The word 'tradition' is a dangerous word, as John Henry Newman, the prime mover in the Oxford Movement and of Anglo-Catholicism found. It is infinitely safer to keep to the Scriptures. But at this point we must face the second matter which arises naturally under this heading, the problem of interpreting and expounding. This is, possibly, the most difficult problem for Protestantism. I was amazed to read this: 'Therefore, it is the Church which has the authority to expound the Scriptures'. That is downright popery, a point which was refuted by all the Protestant fathers, including the Anglican fathers. For Bishop John Jewell in his famous book *An Apology*, or *Answer in Defence of the Church of England* and his *Defence of the Apology*,[1] it is not the church, nor the councils of the church, which has the ultimate authority in exposition, but the written works of the Early Church and the Patristic Fathers. To these Richard Hooker added human reason, as is clearly seen in his words quoted by ATD.

My position on the matter is the same as Calvin's, the Puritans, the Methodist fathers, etc. Although the Scriptures demonstrate themselves as being of divine origin, that which convinces us of their truth and which enables us to understand them and to explain them is the internal witness of the Holy Spirit (*Testimonium Spiritus Internum*). But to protect ourselves from heresy, and to support our own opinions we have the works of the Fathers. That is why Luther and Calvin used to refer so much to Augustine and others; but not, let us note, as final authorities as Jewell and Hooker, and especially the Anglo-Catholics, use them. By today, of course, we have the commentaries of Luther and Calvin themselves, not to mention the Puritans and many other later authors. That is the reason for the words which amaze ATD – 'consulting others by reading and speaking' (I had already taken so much advantage of your space, Mr Editor, that I could not venture to enlarge upon that).

---

[1] See *The Works of John Jewell,* (repr. Cambridge: The Parker Society), 'The Third Portion' (1848), and 'The Fourth Portion' (1850).

Authority in respect of 'the laying down of Rituals and Ceremonies, and authority in disputes concerning the Faith' (Article xx,
which was quoted by ATD) is a completely different matter. At
this point the creeds and confessions come in. Between even them
the big question is, who has the authority to act finally in such
matters? For the Anglican Church this authority lies in Parliament
as was seen with the new Book of Common Prayer measure in
1928. But who has the authority to pronounce what should be
believed? The present-day situation proclaims clearly that to
join the Episcopal Church does not solve the problem. Take, for
example, the present wranglings between the Archbishop of
Canterbury and the Bishop of Woolwich. Who is to decide who is
right? Is there a way to discipline a bishop who has been ordained
to be a father to his people, a shepherd to the sheep and a keeper to
watch over the Faith, when (according to his own archbishop) he
rejects the clear teaching of the Bible and the creeds? Once again,
what union can there be between the Catholic element and the
evangelical element in the Church of England? From week to
week, as we see in our papers, they continually contradict each
other completely in their conferences and congregations, I
regularly read articles by my friend, Dr J. I. Packer and others,
articles which attack the majority in the Anglican Church in terms
of their being wholly unscriptural, and out of touch with the
Articles and the Book of Common Prayer, in their ideas concerning bishops, the sacraments, and the way of salvation, etc.
There is no authority within Anglicanism. Indeed, there is more
confusion, disorder and a breaking of rules within that church than
any other of the religious bodies.

The Situation Today
It would be easy, but totally worthless to quote an anonymous
person who would try to imagine what Luther would say if he
were to return to the world today. Everyone could do that. The
thing we know for certain is that which Luther said of the Church
of Rome in his day, and the fact that Rome boasts that she never
changes ('*Semper Eadem*'). Apart from a few minor points, it cannot
change, because of its nature and belief.

And this is the situation today. Wales is quickly turning into paganism and is becoming papist – What is there to do? Talk about sacraments? No, the great need is for strong preaching which convicts through the power of the Holy Spirit, to pronounce judgment, to call for repentance, to offer salvation which is free through the blood of Christ, justification through faith alone, and a miraculous rebirth. But one must believe these truths and be sure of them before we can pray for the outpouring of the Holy Spirit which only can assist us to hold back the threatening flood.

I shall be very pleased if this discussion between my old friend[1] and myself will be of any help to point all our minds towards the basic truths.

D. Martyn Lloyd-Jones

The Unity of Evangelical Churches

39 Mount Park Crescent,
Ealing, London W. 5
5 February, 1965

[To the Rev. Graham S. Harrison][2]
Dear Mr Harrison,

Many thanks for your kind letter and for the copy of your statement on 'The Church'. I think that this is excellent. It reads really well and I believe puts the main issues before us. I have

[1] It is worthy of note that ML-J was often able to retain some friendship with men with whom he disagreed as strongly as he did with ATD. On hearing of ML-J's illness in 1968, ATD started a letter to Mrs Lloyd-Jones with the words: 'Dear Bethan, I heard from Ieuan last night that Dr Martyn is in hospital and that he has undergone surgery. Would you remember us very warmly to him, and wish him a speedy recovery . . .'

[2] Mr Harrison, Baptist pastor at Newport, Gwent, was working with two colleagues in the Evangelical Movement of Wales, to produce a statement which would bring evangelical congregations of different denominational background into closer unity. This letter is ML-J's response to the draft. After further work on the statement (see below), it was published as a booklet entitled *The Christian Church* (Bridgend: Evangelical Movement of Wales, 1966).

therefore nothing but minor criticisms to offer.

1.   I feel that under the heading of 'The Task of the Church' on pages 5 and 6 you should include the administration of the Sacraments, or, if you prefer it, the observance of the Ordinances.

2.   First para. page 15.   I am not happy about the statement which suggests that because we are not all agreed in our interpretation of the Word of God as spoken authoritatively that we are suggesting that He has therefore spoken ambiguously.   This does not follow at all, and we are not thereby 'foisting our spiritual obtuseness upon God and His Word'.   Otherwise, as I have already said, I think it is excellent, and you have handled the question of 'Baptism' in as perfect a manner as I can imagine.

With my kindest regards,
Yours very sincerely,
    D. M. Lloyd-Jones

On Leaving a Denomination

39 Mount Park Crescent,
Ealing, London W.5
12 April, 1965

[To the Rev. C. M. Hilton Day][1]
Dear Mr Hilton Day,

I am truly grateful to you for your most kind letter and your reactions to the Conference.[2] I find these to be most valuable.

With regard to your main feeling about what should be done at the present time, I have just to say that I am in entire agreement with you. I have all along felt that it is wrong simply to call men

---

[1] Charles M. Hilton Day (1910–75), was minister of the English Presbyterian Church at Silloth in Cumbria. Ordained in 1936, he mourned the decline of biblical Christianity in his denomination which merged into the United Reformed Church soon after his retirement in 1972. The right time for secession was being discussed by a number of men at this date.

[2] The third Leicester Ministers' Conference which had met in early April.

out without having thought the matter right through. In any case these matters are never to be done in cold blood, there must always be some very definite leading and sense of constraint. I am sure that we need to exercise great patience in this extremely complex situation in which we find ourselves, and I am sure that at the end we shall be shown the way.

I cannot tell you how much I feel for people situated as you are, and it grieves me much to think that I cannot be of more active and positive help.

May I also say how much I valued your presence at the Conference. It meant much more than you can well realize. Some of the younger men have never really had to face the true position as it is and are therefore liable to jump to conclusions based on purely theoretical considerations.

May God greatly bless you and your good lady and grant you much peace of mind and heart and encouragement in your labours.

With warm greetings,
Yours sincerely,
   D. M. Lloyd-Jones

The London Baptist Association and Church Unity

49 Creffield Road,
Ealing, London W.5
28 August, 1965

[To the Rev. Kenneth Howard]
Dear Mr Howard,

Many many thanks for your kindness in sending me the enclosed and allowing me to see it.[1]

I must confess that it leaves me much where I was. What amazes me is that no one seems to be facing the problem from the standpoint of evangelical unity. It is always a negative reaction,

[1] Kenneth Howard (1921–92), Baptist pastor at East Ham, London, had sent ML-J an account of a meeting of the London Baptist Association (20 July 1965), convened, along with provincial meetings, to discuss the resolutions on church unity passed at the Nottingham Faith and Order

coupled with a failure and even a refusal to face the position they are already in.[1]

However, I must try to be patient.

It was a great joy and privilege to listen to you that night at Wappenham and to have fellowship with you.[2]

My wife joins me in warm regards to you both,

Yours very sincerely,

D. M. Lloyd-Jones

Conference in 1964. The purpose of the discussions was to enable the Council of the Baptist Union to state the attitude of the denomination to the unity question. The Union's statement, published in 1967, included the significant words: 'When in 1888 the members of the Baptist Union assembly sought to bring the Down Grade Controversy to an end, they expressly disavowed and disallowed any power to control belief or restrict inquiry.' It also concluded that to press for organic unity by 1980 (as the Nottingham resolutions had urged) would 'endanger denominational unity'. *Baptists and Unity* (Baptist Union of Great Britain and Ireland: London, n.d.), pp. 30, 50.

[1] While the account sent by Howard revealed no general desire for a move among Baptists towards unity with other churches, a concern for Baptist unity clearly took precedence over concerted action with other evangelicals for a wider unity which would oppose ecumenism. Many professing evangelicals saw no real danger in ecumenism, taking the view expressed by the Rev. M. H. Cressey who said of the 'trends' in the ecumenical movement ('overconcentration on social concerns, blurring of theological issues, and a drift to compromise with the unreformed Church of Rome') 'that these trends are more apparent than real and that in so far as they have reality they are as actively opposed within the ecumenical movement as they are from outside it' (*Evangelicals and Unity: Nottingham Before and After,* ed., J. D. Douglas [Abingdon: Marcham Manor Press: 1964], p. 26). In this spirit one Baptist leader, the Rev. Hubert W. Janisch, wrote to ML-J on 20 March 1967, 'A different attitude from yours towards the Ecumenical Movement does not necessarily mean for one moment a weakening of Evangelical conviction.' Janisch also said, 'I am to be Moderator of the Free Church Federal Council, which is Protestant and Evangelical.' In contrast with such an optimistic assessment, ML-J believed that 'Christianity is fighting for its life'.

[2] For the discussion which took place between them on unity at Wappenham see *D. Martyn Lloyd-Jones: The Fight of Faith,* pp. 507–8. Howard subsequently left the Baptist Union.

Anticipation of a Crisis

49 Creffield Road,
Ealing, London W.5
21 December, 1965

[To Dr Philip E. Hughes]

My dear Philip,

I cannot tell you how truly delighted I was to receive your letter of the 12th. I had intended writing to you at this point in any case in addition to the usual card of greetings, but you have forestalled me once more.

I have been having an exceptionally busy time travelling in various parts of the country as well as my work at Westminster. The position here is still very confused and I am sure that we are heading up during this next year to a real crisis on what is to me the fundamental issue, namely do we believe in a territorial church or in a gathered church of saints? [1] You will know about or seen the symposium edited by Packer – 'All in Each Place'.[2] This I think indicates clearly the dividing points between evangelicals. Some of us cannot understand this attitude to make accommodations for 'The Anglo-Catholic conscience', for that is surely to make accommodation for 'another Gospel which is not a Gospel'. However, I must not pursue this in a letter.

I gather that the position is something similar out there with evangelicals increasingly prepared to compromise on the Scriptures

---

[1] He saw inevitable division between 'a congregation of faithful men, in which the pure Word of God is preached . . .' (Article xix of the 39 Articles) and congregations and denominations content to include as members all who merely *profess* to be Christian. The Anglican evangelical policy, which developed in contrast to his, adopted the essentially ecumenical position in its statement: 'We believe that the visible unity of all professing Christians should be our goal'. *The Nottingham Statement* (London: Falcon, 1977), p. 45.

[2] *All in Each Place: Towards Reunion in England, Ten Anglican Essays with some Free Church Comment,* ed., J. I. Packer (Abingdon: Marcham Manor Press, 1965).

[167]

and on other matters. It is to me nothing less than tragic that evangelicals do not see that they have a unique opportunity at the present time if they but stood together. They still fondly imagine that they can infiltrate the various bodies to which they belong and win them over. What you report in your letter is really the answer to that.

I am glad to say that Hodder & Stoughton kindly sent me a copy of your book at the time of its publication and I have greatly enjoyed reading it. I am very touched by the fact that you even thought of dedicating it to me. I would have regarded that as a real privilege. I am sure that it is going to do great good.

I was reading in the *English Churchman* yesterday a review of a book in which the reviewer said that apart from works by you and Leon Morris that evangelicals have failed to produce any big books of substance and of lasting value, and this is undoubtedly true.

I was very glad indeed to read of how you are settling there and to know that there are prospects of your being over next summer. We shall be out of the country from mid-July to mid-August but shall be somewhere in England during the latter part of August and early September; so please let me know your exact plans as soon as they materialise.

Please notice my new address. Ann got married last April and we have moved to this house where Ann and her husband occupy the upper flat and Bethan and I the lower flat.

We all join in sending much love to you three and our warmest good wishes for the New Year and always.

Yours very sincerely,
D. M. Lloyd-Jones

Further Comment on the Unity
of Evangelical Churches[1]

Westminster Chapel,
Buckingham Gate,
London S.W.1
25 January, 1966

[To the Rev. Graham S. Harrison]

Dear Mr Harrison,

Please forgive me for this delay in writing to you but as you know Christmas came immediately after the Puritan Conference, then I was away for a while and had a cold and somehow mislaid your MS. But I have now read it and write to congratulate you on what I regard as a really first-class effort. It seems to me to be just the thing that is desired and I have only a few minor criticisms and suggestions, they are as follows:-

On page 6 the paragraph beginning with the words 'In summary then' I feel that the sentence starting with the words 'At the same time' is not quite clear. I had to re-read it to see the meaning. That is a purely mechanical point of course.

Page 7 the middle paragraph beginning with the words 'In the New Testament churches'. I wonder whether it would be well to omit 'full-time' from the sentence beginning 'Some of the elders'.

Page 8 second paragraph beginning with the word 'Finally.' I feel that in the sentence beginning 'First of all' that in addition to 'Doctrine' at the end you should add 'and Spirit'. Then at the bottom of that page I feel that you have not dealt sufficiently with the doctrine of the Father. You deal specially with 'Jesus Christ' and with 'the Holy Spirit' and surely it is a part of our Reformed tradition to give at least equal emphasis to the Father specifically.

Page 10 No. 8. When I began to read the paragraph 'Yet we admit' and came to the question of 'the interpretation of prophecy' I immediately put a query in the margin as to whether this should be included. Then I found, of course, that you yourself dealt with

---

[1] Comment on the final draft of the material to be included in *The Christian Church*.

that and pointed out that it has never caused a division in the Church. I feel therefore that it would be wiser to omit this altogether as it is not really relevant to the issue that is before us.

Page 11 No. 8, Subsection 1. Should not the 'mode' of Baptism be included also? I find constantly that people are concerned about this. I myself only baptize adult believers but by sprinkling, so I feel the question of the mode should be included.

Page 12 No. 8, Subsection (c): 'Rebaptism'. You refer to 'being allowed to receive it'. The difficulty that is likely to arise is if Baptists 'insist' upon their receiving it. That is much more likely in my opinion to cause trouble than the other.

But as I say, these are only minor criticisms and I again congratulate you on a really excellent bit of work.

With my warmest regards,

Yours very sincerely,

D. M. Lloyd-Jones

Membership of The Westminster Fellowship

49 Creffield Road,
Ealing, London W.5
10 December, 1966

[To the Rev. David N. Samuel]¹

Dear Mr Samuel,

How very kind of you to write to me. I appreciate it very much indeed.

I assure you that what I felt constrained to do about the Fellowship has been most grievous to me and yet I have felt, as you know,

¹ The Rev. David N. Samuel, Vicar of Ravendale, Lincolnshire (subsequently Director of Church Society and incumbent at St Mary's, Reading), who had joined the monthly fraternal of ministers which met under ML-J's chairmanship at Westminster Chapel in 1964. At the November 1966 meeting ML-J had dissolved the original Fellowship on the grounds that disagreement on the subject of the ecumenical movement, and its relationship to denominational loyalties, was occurring so often that the meetings were being impeded. He wanted a new Fellowship whose members were convinced that adherence to the gospel

for some considerable time that this was the only thing to do.

I am sorry to find that the impression seems to have been given in the afternoon meeting that only men who were prepared to leave their denominations immediately could attend the new Fellowship. This is certainly not my idea. I feel that the only people who should be excluded from it are those who are convinced denominationalists and who feel that evangelicals must always stay in the larger bodies. Otherwise it is quite open. I should be very grieved if the fellowship between people like you and myself were broken, but I do feel that the rigid denominationalists are really excluding themselves.

With all good wishes,

Yours very sincerely,

D. M. Lloyd-Jones

Denominations and a 'World Church': a 'turning point in history'

Westminster Chapel,
Buckingham Gate,
London S.W.1
1 January, 1967

[To the Members of Westminster Chapel, 1967]

Dear Friend,

In the middle of my 29th year here at Westminster it is my privilege once more to write a word of greeting to you.

Looking back across these years I naturally see many changes and

---

had to come before any denominational commitment. He was deliberately not present at the afternoon session in November when the new terms for membership were discussed. Although Dr Samuel remained in the Church of England ministry (until the 1990s) he continued, along with others in that denomination, as he informs me, 'to enjoy close fellowship with Dr Lloyd-Jones until his death'. And adds: 'He was a man who found true fellowship with those who knew the true gospel and loved and served the Lord Jesus Christ, wherever they were situated.'

yet the feeling uppermost in my mind is one of the remarkable continuity of which I am aware.

My difficulty this time is to know what to select out of the many things in my mind and heart. Of all these in my opinion the most vitally important is the relationship between the local church and the general situation.

There is always the danger of living only to ourselves, and for ourselves, in the local church. While that must ever remain our chief concern we must not stop at that. We are part of a larger whole, and we are responsible for what happens there also. Failure to realise this accounts for much of the confusion at the present time. This applies to all sections of the Christian Church. The feeling too often is that as long as we are happy and all is going well with us locally that nothing else matters. But we cannot contract out of our responsibilities in that way.

The year 1966 has reminded us of that very forcibly and more so than ever before. It has been an astonishing year which has witnessed momentous events. Among them are the following. Last May the great majority of Congregational Churches in this country covenanted together to form the Congregational Church of England. We refused to do so for the reasons with which you are familiar. As if to confirm the rightness of our decision the following events have also taken place. For the first time since the Protestant Reformation a Roman Catholic priest has preached in Westminster Abbey, the Archbishop of Canterbury has paid an official visit to the Pope, a united procession of all the churches of Westminster (apart from ourselves and the Baptist Church in Horseferry Road) marched from Trafalgar Square to the Roman Catholic Cathedral for a joint service at which the Scriptures were read by a Free Church minister, prayers were read by an Anglican minister, and the sermon was preached by Cardinal Heenan. On top of all this a meeting was held in June at St. Martin-in-the-Fields at which representatives of all the 'world religions' took part. All these and many other less publicised meetings and conferences are but moves in the direction of the formation of a 'World Church' including the Roman Catholics.

It was in the light of all this that I made an appeal, at a meeting held in the Westminster Central Hall in October, to all truly Evangelical people in all the denominations to come together and to form local independent Evangelical churches which should be in a loose fellowship together in order that the world might hear and see a living witness to the truth of the Gospel.

What of the future? Our duty is clear. We must continue to maintain our life and regular witness to the truth of the Gospel in all ways. As the Apostle Paul reminds the Philippians we are set for 'the defence and confirmation of the Gospel', and are meant to 'strive together for the faith of the Gospel'.

But we must not do that in isolation. As 'no man liveth unto himself' no church can live unto herself. It is our duty to be in close fellowship with all similar and like-minded churches and to do all we can to help them and encourage them and enrich their lives in all ways. They in turn will help us. It has already been our privilege to be of some help to churches which, because of their loyalty to the 'Truth', have suffered financially. We hope not only to continue this but greatly to increase it.

We intend in the annual business meeting of the church on Thursday, 16th March next to consider the question of our formal relationship to such churches, and I hereby give notice of that.

We are living in momentous times, undoubtedly one of the great turning-points of history. The opportunity for Evangelical witness is unique, the possibilities are tremendous. Are we equal to the times?

May God enable us to realise these things and to be aware of the privilege of our position, and the high responsibility that rests upon us. But above all may He enable us to rise to this 'high calling'.

We thank God for the memory of all who have gone 'to be with Christ' and offer again our deep sympathy to their loved ones who remain to mourn their loss.

We welcome all who receive this letter for the first time who have joined us during the past year.

May the Holy Spirit shine upon the Word and in our hearts more and more, building us up and making us strong to fight the battles of the Lord.

[173]

As we end one year and start another what can we say but 'Blessed be the God and Father of our Lord Jesus Christ, who hath blessed us with all spiritual blessings in heavenly places in Christ' (Ephesians i, 3).

With an increasing sense of the high privilege of being called, and enabled in a measure, to serve you in the Gospel,

I remain,

Yours in the bonds of Christ,

    D. M. Lloyd-Jones

Did Calvin Practise Secession?

49 Creffield Road
Ealing, London W.5
11 April, 1967

[To Dr Philip E. Hughes]

Dear Philip,

I cannot tell you how delighted I was to see you on Sunday and to have that chat with you though it was so brief.

I am most grateful also for your allowing me to see and to read the enclosed MS. I much enjoyed it and find myself in substantial agreement. I think the Calvin quotations are liable to some misunderstanding as he was really dealing with the wild sectarians who were breaking away from the Church without any adequate reason. Otherwise his words can only mean that it was a mistake to leave the Roman Catholic Church, something which he himself had done.

I also feel that the only real logical conclusion to arrive at from your tremendous climax is 'Come out from among them and be ye separate' (Rev. 18.4). That is the only way, surely, in which we can make a truly effective protest against what is happening. Merely to pass resolutions and raise objections and then to abide by majority decisions is being proved to be valueless, and the authorities in control are well aware of this. However, I must not pursue this matter.

I do hope that we shall be able to arrange to meet in the summer.

With my warmest regards as ever,

Yours very sincerely,

    D. M. Lloyd-Jones

Counsel in Discouraging Days

49 Creffield Road,
Ealing, London W.5
10 November, 1967

[To the Rev. Graham S. Harrison]

Dear Mr Harrison,

Many thanks for your most kind letter. It was very good of you to write and I am much encouraged by what you say.

With regard to my address on Luther, I am hoping to publish this.[1] I have not quite decided as yet whether to publish it alone or with something else, but probably it will be alone. I am persuaded that what you say is right.

With regard to your position as regards the Baptist Union, I entirely agree with what you say. I have always said that it is better for men not to act in isolation but rather to wait until a number can act together. We seem to have gone back on that during the last year or so, but we must always allow for the individual conscience in this matter.

With regard to the question of preaching, I find it much more difficult to know what to say. I am sure that your concern about this is the real key to the solution. More and more I have found that the preparation of myself is the most important factor. The danger is to be tied either to one's manuscript or else to one's

---

[1] He had spoken on 'Luther and his Message' at the first British Evangelical Council conference to be held at Westminster Chapel (31 October–1 November 1967) and it was published by The Evangelical Press (London: 1968).

preparation, and forget the 'freedom of the Spirit'. We must talk about this sometime, although as I have always said, I have never been able to lecture on this subject: but by means of question and answer I think something might be done.[1]

We are living of course in most discouraging days and you must beware that the devil does not cast you down.

With my warmest regards,

Yours very sincerely,

      D. M. Lloyd-Jones

The Change for the Worse among Evangelicals

Westminster Chapel,
Buckingham Gate,
London S.W.1
1 January, 1968

[To the Members of Westminster Chapel, 1968]

Dear Friend,

As I send yet another Annual Letter and word of greeting to you at the beginning of a New Year I am more conscious than ever of the distinction drawn in the New Testament between the Christian Church in its general and universal aspect and in its local manifestations in a particular church. What makes me particularly conscious of this at the present time is the striking difference between the two as far as I am concerned in my personal experience. Indeed I thank God for the difference.

As far as we are concerned at Westminster Chapel, by the grace of God we have so much for which we can be truly thankful. I am more than ever conscious of a deep seriousness among us and an ever increasing desire to know God and to serve Him. This is something which many visitors notice, and discuss with me when they come into my vestry at the close of a service. A letter recently from an American doctor serving in Vietnam testified to

---

[1] Happily more than this was done. See below pp. 181n, 219, 221.

the fact that she had been more conscious of the presence of God while worshipping with us for several months than anywhere else, and that amidst the horrors of war she was helped and sustained by the memory of this.

This leads to a sense of oneness and a sense of high purpose which control everything. Nothing can be more encouraging to any preacher than to feel that people come to the services, not out of habit or a sense of duty, but with a deep desire to worship God and to get to know more of Him through our Lord and Saviour. The sense of expectancy can actually be felt – and again visitors sense this.

As a direct result of this there is also the desire for the salvation of others. I have been told at times that certain critics have said of me, 'Oh! he just preaches to a group of people who agree with him'. The fallacies in that statement are staggering. The Church after all is not a debating society, and these critics are the very people who are always talking about unity! But, furthermore, the statement is a lie. Constantly I am being told not only of individual non-Christians who are attending on Sunday nights, but sometimes of even groups of such. But above all I have had the regular experience of welcoming such friends at the close of services, and hearing from their own lips of how they had been brought to a knowledge of salvation.

Thus I find myself greatly encouraged, and thank God for His goodness in calling me to minister to people who are so concerned about His glory and the extension of His Kingdom.

When one turns to the more general position however, the situation is very different. Here, the main impression is one of confusion, uncertainty, and divided opinions. This is true not only in this country but throughout the world. This is something that one expects in 'Christendom', but in the past it has not been true of those calling themselves evangelical. This is the new feature which is so disturbing. No longer can it be assumed that to be evangelical means to accept the authority of the Scriptures on matters of history, and on the creation of the world and man, and at the very lowest to be sceptical about the theory of evolution. In the same way there has been a recrudescence of denominationalism and an entirely new attitude towards Romanism. Institutions which for almost a hundred years have been regarded as bulwarks of orthodoxy are being divided by what is called 'the new thinking', which, in fact, is but some of the old heresies in a new garb.

It is, alas, a time of conflict and of trial, indeed a time of tragedy when old comrades in arms are now in different camps. It is not that one in any way questions the honesty or the sincerity of such friends. There is only one explanation and that is, 'an enemy hath done this'. Never has that enemy been more active or more subtle.

Each one of us has to be loyal to his or her convictions and conscience, and we must align ourselves with all who are like-minded. To that end, as you will know, we have joined The Fellowship of Independent Evangelical Churches during the past year, and through them The British Evangelical Council.

With them it will be our privilege to continue in the good old fight for The Faith. What the outcome of the present upheaval will be no one can tell. Our duty is to be faithful knowing that the final outcome is sure.

During the past year we bade farewell to the Rev. H. M. Carson on his departure to be minister of the Baptist Church in Bangor, Co. Down, Northern Ireland. We shall ever be grateful for the fellowship and co-operation of such a faithful and courageous contender for The Faith.

We have welcomed as his successor the Rev. Edwin E. King, and he has already settled happily among us. He will continue in the same tradition.

During the past year we have seen the passing of a number of dear friends and fellow-members. They will be greatly missed not only by their nearest and dearest but by all of us who knew them. 'Blessed are the dead who die in the Lord.' We thank God for them and for all they meant to us in terms of loyalty and encouragement. May their loved ones know the full 'comfort and consolation of the Scriptures'.

I send a special word of greeting to all who joined our fellowship during 1967.

'Onward, then, ye people,
Join our happy throng, Blend with ours your voices
In the triumph song; Glory, praise, and honour
Unto Christ the King, This through countless ages
Men and angels sing.'

With my warmest greetings and prayers for the prosperity of
your soul and body in 1968 and always,
Yours in the bonds of peace,
D. M. Lloyd-Jones

Chairmanship of the BEC Council

49 Creffield Road,
Ealing, London W.5
11 October, 1968

[To the Rev. Elwyn Davies]
My dear friend,
Many thanks for your letter. We have both been away from
home.
I find it very difficult to know what to tell you this time. My
feeling is that it is rather soon for yourself or for anyone from Wales
to become President of the BEC. The BEC is too small up to now
and the Movement's connection with it too new. If you accepted,
Welsh people could have grounds for believing that you were part
of another movement and those who belong to the Evangelical
Alliance to believe that the BEC was short of resources! In two or
three years time Lamb's[1] intention would be excellent, but, as I've
said, I am not sure that it would be wise now.
Very warm regards, as always,
D. M. Lloyd-Jones

[1] The Rev. The Hon. Roland Lamb was General Secretary of the BEC
from 1967 until 1982.

Controversy over 'Growing into Union'

49 Creffield Road,
Ealing, London W.5
17 September, 1970

[To Dr David Samuel]

My dear Friend,

I feel I must write to you.

Elizabeth Braund kindly allowed me to see what you had sent to her on the book *Growing into Union*.[1] I write simply to say that what you have written fills me with admiration. So many of the reviews, I have felt, have been inadequate; but this is simply first class and gets down to the real issues in an unanswerable manner.

I want to thank you for it but I also want to make a suggestion. This article is so important that while I think it should be published in the *Evangelical Magazine* I feel very strongly that it should have a much wider circulation also. I feel sure that the *Church of England Newspaper* people would be glad to print it. Can I urge you to send it to them also? I write this entirely on my own responsibility and without consulting Elizabeth Braund; but I am sure she will agree.

You really must write more. You not only have a clear brain but also the power of clear expression; and above all you can think theologically. I cannot refrain from saying that I feel strongly that

---

[1] The publication of this book, with its sub-title, *Proposals for Forming a United Church in England* (SPCK: London, May 1970) had led to serious controversy, including a breach in public co-operation between Dr J. I. Packer and ML-J. The work, compiled by two Anglo-Catholics and two evangelicals (Packer and C. O. Buchanan), represented a new alliance and, in Samuel's words, showed how evangelicals had 'succumbed to the popular clamour for pluralism in belief and practice'. Samuel's review (*Evangelical Magazine*, November 1970) also demonstrated that this was not, as some represented it, simply an Anglican-Nonconformist divide. See *D. Martyn Lloyd-Jones: The Fight of Faith*, pp. 656–58, 793–4.

what was once said of Bishop Butler applies equally to you. You may recall that George II, I believe, once asked someone, 'Is Bishop Butler dead?' to which the reply was, 'No, he is not dead but is buried somewhere in the country'!

With my warmest regards,

Yours sincerely,

D. M. Lloyd-Jones

P.S. A still better suggestion! Add to what you have already written sections dealing also with the view of bishops and baptismal regeneration taught in the book and then publish it as a booklet. There will be no difficulty in getting a publisher. D. ML-J.

Thoughts of Westminster Seminary.
Continuing Controversy in England

49 Creffield Road
Ealing, London W.5
22 December, 1970

[To Dr Philip E. Hughes]

My Dear Philip,

We were delighted to receive your letter written on the 16th this morning and to have some news of you.

I am glad you are settling so happily at Westminster.[1] I felt sure that this would be the case. I am sure that you are going to do great work there.

I am glad also to know that you are getting on with your Commentary on Hebrews.[2] I am greatly looking forward to seeing

---

[1] Hughes had moved to teaching posts in the United States in the 1960s and more recently had become visiting professor of New Testament at Westminster Theological Seminary, Philadelphia. ML-J had been at the Seminary the previous year when he had delivered the lectures subsequently published as *Preaching and Preachers*.

[2] When finally published as *A Commentary on the Epistle to the Hebrews* (Grand Rapids: W. B. Eerdmans, 1977) it carried the dedication: 'For Martyn Lloyd-Jones, speaker of the word of God, in gratitude for the constancy of his friendship during more than thirty-five years.'

this when it appears. It will be a real contribution I know.

The first volume of my sermons on the Romans has just appeared. I will send you a copy after Christmas.

I can well picture you working away in your room at the Library at the Seminary. Van Til's room was at my disposal last year. I am particularly fond of Arthur Kuschke.[1] He is a very nice man and improves with knowing tremendously. I found him very helpful.

I quite agree with you about Marcus Loane.[2] I have heard that he has expressed astonishment at what he found to be the attitude of Anglican Evangelicals in this country, both to the ecumenical movement and to Rome. The only developments I have heard of the Packer-Mascall front is that they are bringing out another book in the Spring. There have been several drastic reviews of the previous book, one written by a man who was once an Anglo-Catholic, name David Samuel. This has been printed in the *Evangelical Magazine*. I suppose you saw one letter by Edward Houghton in the *Church of England Newspaper* in September. He is a good Methodist fellow. I have also seen a review written by Klaas Runia which is very critical indeed. This may appear also in the *Evangelical Magazine*. Stibbs is very upset about it all. I hear that most other Anglican Evangelicals are content to do nothing at all about it and just carry on.

As far as I am concerned there was no Puritan Conference this year for the first time.[3] I felt that it would be a farce in the light of that book to continue, for I felt that such concessions had been made to the Catholics that our friend was no more either Evangelical or Puritan. That was not my own personal opinion only but the unanimous feeling of all the Free Church men.

---

[1] The Rev. Arthur Kushke, Librarian at the Seminary.

[2] Archbishop of Sydney, known for his evangelical commitment.

[3] It had been an annual event since 1950. A very similar conference, 'The Westminster Conference', was started under his chairmanship in 1971 but excluding speakers who favoured ecumenical or Anglo-Catholic co-operation.

We think of you often and are still most grateful for all your kindness to us last year. It really made a very vital difference to us. With much love to you three from us all.

Yours ever sincerely,

D. M. Lloyd-Jones

Attitude to the Baptist Union

49 Creffield Road,
Ealing, London W.5
22 October, 1973

[To the Rev. Alan Francis][1]

Dear Mr Francis,

Many thanks for your kind letter of the 11th and the invitation to preach at the 150th Anniversary services at Mount Pleasant.

I have delayed replying in order that I might think this matter through and seek guidance concerning it.

I have come to the reluctant conclusion that I cannot promise to do this. The real reason for this is that I am in trouble over the whole matter of an evangelical church still belonging to the Baptist Union. That is of course for you to decide, but as I am very pledged to support those who have left the Baptist Union I feel that I would be unfair to them to give the impression that this is an indifferent matter. I need say no more and I am sure that you will understand, and also Mr Morris.

With kind regards and greetings,

Yours sincerely,

D. M. Lloyd-Jones

---

[1] Pastor of Mount Pleasant Baptist Church, Swansea.

8

QUERIES AND CONTROVERSIES

Church and Public Mind

Westminster Chapel,
London
19 March, 1947

[The Editor of the *Glasgow Herald*]¹ [1]

Sir,

With reference to the report of the meeting held at St. Andrew's Halls on Tuesday night in connection with the Lord's Day Observance Association of Scotland, I regret to observe a serious error in your report of my address.

You say that I said that the Church 'would require to make full use of the press, the cinema and the wireless,' the reason being that 'these media had more effect on the mind of man than any system of education.'

I certainly made the latter observation, but most definitely not the first.

I bemoaned and regretted the fact that the public mind and mentality are so controlled and determined by the press, the cinema and the wireless. Far from advocating that the Church should therefore use these agencies, I stressed repeatedly that her main task is to counteract their nefarious influence by the preaching of the Gospel; which is the Word of God, the only view of life

---

[1] ML-J was in Glasgow for four meetings on March 18–19, 1947. The meeting on the evening of the 18th was the centenary celebration of the Lord's Day Observance Society of Scotland. The preacher's comment, despite the address, was actually written in Glasgow on March 19 for it was printed in the newspaper of March 20.

that is up to date and offers a reasonable explanation of the world and its present condition, the only hope for a sad and disillusioned age.

I shall be grateful if you will kindly print this correction.

I am, etc.

D. M. Lloyd-Jones

Evangelical Christianity Means More than Calvinism

39 Mount Park Crescent,
Ealing, London W.5
March, 1953

[To the Editor of the *British Weekly*][1]

Sir,

As a regular reader of the *British Weekly*, I confess that I was amazed to find that you deemed it worth your while to give such prominence to a consideration of my little pamphlet on *Maintaining the Evangelical Faith Today*.

I deeply appreciate your understanding of the spirit in which I spoke when I delivered the address of which the pamphlet is a report, and I am truly grateful to you for emphasising that repeatedly in your article. You are good enough to make it quite clear

---

[1] This letter was occasioned by an article in the editorial column of the *British Weekly* for 19 March 1953 which used ML-J's published address to IVF students on *Maintaining the Evangelical Faith Today* (London: IVF, 1952) to attack the whole movement of those who made the authority of Scripture decisive for the Christian Faith. The anonymous writer (Dr Nathaniel Micklem) clearly regarded Lloyd-Jones as the man principally responsible for the opposition to the non-doctrinal Christianity which 'charitably' credited all professing Christians with a portion of the truth. When ML-J's *The Plight of Man and the Power of God* (London: Hodder and Stoughton, 1942) was published, he had reported to Philip Hughes (29 September 1942): 'The reviews have been rather amusing. One friend said that the reviews in *The Times Literary Supplement* and the *British Weekly* reminded him forcibly of men handling a delayed-action high explosive bomb! The IVF's refusal to co-operate with liberals causes intense resentment on the part of the latter.'

that in your opinion I am sincerely and genuinely mistaken, and that I am 'more of a fool than a knave'.

That makes it all the more difficult for me to understand why you dragged in the question of Calvinism and belaboured that point so much. I challenge you to produce any evidence that I have referred to Calvinism either directly or indirectly in my pamphlet. I would not trouble you with this were it not that I know that the great majority of your readers will not have seen the pamphlet and will, therefore, naturally assume that it is nothing but an exposition of what you describe as 'an arbitrary selection from the tenets of Scholastic Calvinism' and that I assert that I cannot co-operate with any who do not agree with this. I do not say that anywhere in the pamphlet, neither have I said or taught it anywhere else or at anytime. To suggest that I, or the IVF, do that is sheer invention; the facts speak roundly to the contrary. I have always asserted and argued as strongly as I could that evangelicals should not separate on the question of Calvinism and Arminianism. They can discuss these matters and disagree about them – but separate concerning them, never. And in fact they do not do so.

In the IVF, both here in Great Britain and on the international level, Arminians and Calvinists work most happily and harmoniously together, and it is my privilege to co-operate with all such. In the same way there are differing schools of thought amongst us about prophecy and the question of the mode or method of sanctification, as well as other matters.

Moreover, I worked for five years in the happiest manner possible with the late Dr G. Campbell Morgan though he and I held opposing views on these matters. Furthermore I have been severely criticised more than once for asking certain well-known Arminians to occupy my pulpit during my summer vacations.

To be 'yet more vile' it will interest you to know that I am denounced as a dangerous Arminian by a Society of Hyper-Calvinists here in London[1] because in my pamphlet on *The*

---

[1] The Sovereign Grace Union, a small publishing organisation which, while re-issuing some good material, had accepted the hyper-Calvinistic position as it had come to prevail among branches of the Strict Baptist churches in the nineteenth century.

Presentation of the Gospel I teach that a free offer of Salvation should be made to all in preaching.

You charge me with 'ascribing motives' to others who support and co-operate with the ecumenical movement. Again I find no evidence for this in the pamphlet. I state, and deal with, the reasons that they give for their actions, but surely that is not to attribute motives. But when you write as you do about me and my pamphlet you are most certainly ascribing and attributing views to me which I do not express in the pamphlet.

I pleaded for the maintaining of that Biblical Evangelical Faith to which Arminians, Lutherans and Calvinists subscribe. That is my position and for that I make no apology.

Neither do I make any apology for the 'ignorance' which hitherto has led me to believe, unlike you, Sir, that there is no 'theological and doctrinal disagreement between St. Paul, St. John and the writer to the Hebrews'.

Again, however, I thank you for the scrupulous fairness, and the kindness, with which you have dealt with the spirit, if not the letter, of my little pamphlet.

D. Martyn Lloyd-Jones

Scientific Knowledge not a Key to Scripture

39 Mount Park Crescent,
Ealing, London W.5
22 September, 1959

[To Professor Donald MacKay]
Dear Dr MacKay,

Many thanks for your most kind and cordial letter.

I hope you are not under the impression that I am spending my time in discussing you!

In my capacity as Chairman of the IVF Advisory Committee this whole question of Science and Religion came up and I illustrated what I was saying in terms of that discussion at the British Council of Churches meeting.[1]

With most of what you say in your letter I am in agreement, but it still does not seem to me to cover the line you were taking that morning. Your exposition then seemed to me, and still does, to depend entirely on your scientific knowledge. That, I contend, is already wrong in principle, and it seems to me extremely dangerous also.

At those meetings I am not concerned to defend any party line, still less am I concerned about what they may think of me.

I am sure that the same applies to you also. The discussions are of value solely in terms of Truth, but nothing could give me greater joy than to know that we are contending for the same things.

My warmest regards,

D. M. Lloyd-Jones

---

[1] ML-J, with a few other evangelicals, had been attending a 'Group on Differing Biblical Presuppositions' which had its first meeting in November 1956. Dr Donald MacCrimmon MacKay (1922–87), who was prominent in the Inter-Varsity movement, had attended on 30 September 1958 and, in the course of discussion on Paul's conversion, had disagreed with ML-J on whether 'a voice . . . speaking in the Hebrew tongue' (Acts 2:14) had to be understood in physical terms, i.e., as 'a vibration of molecules on the eardrum'. While some in the group clearly did not believe that Paul's eyes saw Jesus or that his eardrums heard His word, MacKay seemed to be using scientific insights to support a more mediating position. He argued that an event may be 'real' even though it cannot be recorded by scientific instruments. ML-J's concern was that all claims to 'interpret' Scripture by means of supposed knowledge which lies outside Scripture are dangerous and ultimately (as in this case) destructive of the Bible's own testimony. (British Council of Churches unpublished notes of the ninth meeting of the Group on Differing Biblical Presuppositions. See also *D. Martyn Lloyd-Jones: The Fight of Faith*, pp. 313–20.) In fairness to Dr MacKay's reputation it should be said that in the 1970s, when signs of the weakening in British evangelicalism were more apparent, he stood firm on the orthodox side.

Distinguishing between a Psychological and a Spiritual Problem

39 Mount Park Crescent,
Ealing, London W.5
22 September, 1959

[To the Rev. J. Gwyn-Thomas]

Dear Mr Gwyn-Thomas,

Many thanks for your most kind letter. I am of course only too glad to be of any little help to you and I can well understand how you feel about a difficult case like this.

This is what I feel about the situation. I am sure that you have been dealing with this man on the right lines. At any rate this is the best way possible of determining whether he is primarily a spiritual case or whether it is an essentially psychological problem. What I suggest therefore is this, that having allowed him to talk so much and so freely about the past and about what he thinks about it you should now prohibit him to do this and say that the essence of the Christian position is that the particular form which the past has taken does not matter at all, that what matters now is the present and the future, and that if he is concerned only about his relationship to God and looks to the power and the strength that the Holy Spirit will give him in and through his new nature, he has nothing to fear. In other words you must test him and this will be a good way of deciding whether he is a true believer or not. If he is a true believer he will be ready to reject the past and every voice that comes from it as being the temptation of the devil. I therefore suggest that you try this method and if he should not respond well then you will be justified in assuming that he is essentially a psychological case. Please let me know if I can help you further.

With regard to coming down to your Convention next year I am afraid that at the moment I cannot promise anything definite as my plans are at present uncertain. Please get into touch with me, say round about Christmas, if you can wait until then.

My wife joins me in warmest regards to you both,

Yours very sincerely,

D. M. Lloyd-Jones

Disappointment in the Ministry

National Club,
Pall Mall,
London S.W.1
[undated, perhaps Easter, 1961]

[To Dr Douglas Johnson, at the Close,
Ross-on-Wye, Herefordshire]

My dear Sir,

I send you the enclosed not because I imagine that you have not received it, but because I feel constrained to tell you my reaction to it.[1]

It is that I thank God for you, and your sanity, and your entire freedom from this pathetic self-importance that afflicts so many of our friends and which is encouraged by so many who should know better – I could never have stayed in London.

I am increasingly depressed by it all and if it were not for you I should feel utterly lonely.

My warmest regards to you both.

Yours very sincerely,

D. M. Lloyd-Jones

---

[1] D. J., in supplying this letter to me, could not recall the incident which prompted it, and the 'enclosure' to which it refers was not preserved. It may have been related to the resurgence of Calvinistic belief which was occurring at this time and for which ML-J was being blamed, even within the Inter-Varsity Fellowship. Philip Hughes was among those considered for the post of Warden at the Fellowship's study centre at Cambridge. In a letter to Hughes of 21 July 1960, ML-J wrote: 'We had a meeting of the Advisory Committee of the IVF the other day. As the result of that I am truly delighted that you are not going to Tyndale House. At the moment they seem to have but *one* idea and that is to preserve the unity of the IVF at all costs. There is clearly an anti-reformed activity at the present time. It is really very pathetic, not to say schoolboyish! You are well out of it all!'

The Biography of T. C. Williams

Westminster Chapel,
Buckingham Gate,
London S.W.1
9 June, 1964

[To the Rev. Llewelyn Williams]
Dear Mr Llewelyn Williams,[1]

Many thanks for your most kind letter. I am most interested to hear that you are preparing a biography of Thomas Charles Williams. I have always felt that it should have been done years ago. With regard to your query about the conversation at Crickhowell in 1927,[2] I fear it was in very vague terms. His idea was that I should start and found a kind of order of preaching friars who should go up and down the country preaching and evangelizing. What made him say this was that I had felt a call to work in the Forward Movement rather than in a regular church.

Actually this conversation was a sequel to a previous conversation we had had in August 1926 at the wedding of the eldest daughter of Sir John Morris-Jones to Dr Ernest Jones of Aberystwyth. I was the best man at that wedding and T. C. had taken part in the service with the local minister. I well remember the scene in the garden afterwards when I was standing in a group consisting of Lloyd-George, Ellis Griffiths and, I believe, Sir Robert Thomas and Sir John Morris-Jones, when T. C. Williams came along and taking hold of me said, 'Come with me, you and I have things to talk about that these fellows cannot understand'. He had just heard of my decision to enter the Ministry and on that occasion he warned me to be wary and careful lest the Anglo-Catholics in the Church of England should persuade me to join them and enter one of their orders. I assured him that there was no danger of that as I was far too much a Welshman and a Calvinistic Methodist ever to think of such a thing.

[1] The Rev. Huw Llewelyn Williams, Calvinistic Methodist minister at Valley, Anglesey, who published a biography of the Rev. Thomas Charles Williams (1868–1927) in 1964. Original of this letter in National Library of Wales, C. M. Archives H37/42.

[2] See *D. Martyn Lloyd-Jones: The First Forty Years*, p. 178

T. C. used to preach regularly at Westminster Chapel, first for Campbell Morgan and afterwards for Dr Jowett. I have never been able to get any recollections of him that are of any value. I am afraid that the impression he left upon many was in connection with his vanity. He had a habit, apparently, of turning round when in the pulpit and bowing to the ladies in the choir sitting behind him. I often heard him preach here in those days.

Maddeuwch y Saesneg yma. Nid oes neb yma yn deall Cymraeg.

Cofion caredig,

Yn gywir,

[*Please excuse the English. No one here understands Welsh. Kind Regards*]

    D. M. Lloyd-Jones

The Sufferings of Christ

Westminster Chapel,
Buckingham Gate,
London S.W.1
6 April, 1967

[To Mr L. B. Gunn][1]

Dear Mr Gunn,

Many thanks for your kind letter.

With regard to the point you raise the answer is as follows:

(1) The fact that our Lord was aware of what was to happen before He came to earth does not do away with what He felt in human nature when He came up to the point of crisis and realized with a new intensity what it would involve.

(2) Your suggestion that the incident is to be explained in terms of the devil's activity is surely quite impossible. Our Lord's words in the Garden of Gethsemane, 'nevertheless not my will, but thine,

---

[1] Mr L. B. Gunn of Esher, Surrey, comments to us about this response which he received: 'The great thing is the helpful and kindly way Dr Lloyd-Jones replied to someone completely unknown to him. If he did this to me he must have done so for hundreds of others.'

be done' is more than enough to establish this.

(3) Our Lord was never afraid of the devil and it would be very wrong to suggest that He was or was in any way terrified by him.

(4) There is really no difficulty about the physical phenomenon of sweating blood, and from the standpoint of the main issue which you raise it is but indicative of the intensity of the agony.

I trust this will be of some help to you. As I said on Good Friday morning, there is no satisfactory explanation save the one I gave. It was God who 'gave the cup' to the Son.

With all good wishes,

Yours sincerely,

D. M. Lloyd-Jones

Pentecostalist Controversy and the Need for Discernment

49 Creffield Road,
Ealing, London W.5
28 February, 1969

[To the Rev. Dr John A. Schep][1]

Dear Professor Schep,

Please forgive me for this terrible delay in replying to your most kind letters which you sent on December 16th. I was away from home over Christmas and a little after and have been extremely

---

[1] Dr Schep (1897–1972), emigrated from the Netherlands to Australia and was a founding minister of the Reformed Churches of Australia (1951). He became Professor of New Testament at the denomination's college at Geelong, Victoria, retiring in 1964. In his later years Dr Schep and his wife became involved in what they regarded as a 'revival' in Geelong. He began to teach that the 'baptism of the Spirit' was not something received by all Christians at their regeneration and in writing of his own personal change to ML-J he commented: 'Oh that terrible Dutch pride and intellectualism! Always fighting about doctrinal issues, but hardly any fellowship with each other in prayer and praise.' Schep's testimony and booklet on *The Baptism with the Holy Spirit* caused considerable controversy within his own denomination and he was answered principally by Dr Klaas Runia, Professor of Theology at Geelong. Both sides in the controversy appealed to ML-J.

busy ever since, so that things have got into arrears. I know you will understand.

I certainly read everything you sent most carefully through although I confess it was very difficult to wade through Dr Runia's criticisms and your comments superimposed.

I feel that we are still left very much where we were and I find myself in between both of you. I feel that you perhaps do not 'prove and try the spirits' sufficiently, and that you stress Tongues in the Pentecostal sense and as those who are guilty of the Corinthian error do,[1] whereas I feel that Prof. Runia is guilty of 'quenching the Spirit'. I may say that I have heard from him also and have written to him to that effect.

Do you want me to return Prof. Runia's notes with your comments or not? I should be happy to do so if necessary.

I am continuing to remember you all and praying that God may overrule all to His Glory. What concerns me particularly is that the whole doctrine of the Baptism with the Spirit should not be rejected because of the difficulty over Tongues. That would be to me a tragedy and would tend to delay Revival.

I am once more considering the possibility of trying to publish my sermons on this subject.

I am glad to say that I am well. I have to go to lecture at the Westminster Theological Seminary for six weeks on 'Preaching' on April 14th next.

With loving greetings to you both from my wife and myself,
Yours very sincerely,
    D. M. Lloyd-Jones

---

1 ML-J's position was that there is no necessary connection between the gift of tongues and the baptism of the Spirit: 'In the times of great revival when the Spirit of God has been poured forth and thousands have been baptised with the Spirit, there is generally no mention of their working miracles, no suggestion that they "spake with tongues".' *Romans: An Exposition of Chapter 8:5–17* (Banner of Truth, 1974), p. 305. He was unhappy with Schep's account of tongues and with the professor's belief that all Christians could have the gift – teaching which coincided closely with what was being currently urged in pentecostal and charismatic circles around the world.

Definitions which Leave no Room for Revival

49 Creffield Road,
Ealing, London W.5
28 February, 1969

[To the Rev. Dr Klaas Runia]

Dear Professor Runia,

Many thanks for your letter of the 12th and the enclosed copy of your comments on Prof. Schep's booklets.[1] I have read this with great interest and am very happy indeed to make my comments.

What is so interesting to me once more is, that I find myself in a position between you two.

More in detail:

(1) I certainly feel that Prof. Schep has crossed the line into a form of Pentecostalism. He shows this in his emphasis on Tongues and also in his urging people to seek this particular gift and, indeed, to claim it. I felt in reading his booklets that an obvious struggle was taking place with regard to this but I feel that he has crossed the line.

(2) I still feel that you really do not allow for Revival. You show this in your final paragraph on page 13 where you say, 'Read all the passages that speak of the Holy Spirit in the Church. It is always: 'Become what you are', ALL of you'. If it is simply a question of 'Become what you are' and nothing more, then how can one pray for Revival, and indeed how does one account for the Revivals in the history of the Church?[2]

(3) To me Revival means that which can happen to an individual happening to a number of people or a number of churches at the same time.

[1] Twelve pages of notes were enclosed. The gist of Runia's argument can be followed without our giving his text.

[2] His point is that if a larger giving of the Spirit is not to be expected by individual Christians neither is it by numbers of Christians. Consequently the historic definition of revival (held by Edwards, Whitefield, Spurgeon etc.) as an 'outpouring of the Spirit' upon many at once would have to be abandoned. On this see George Smeaton, *The Doctrine of the Holy Spirit* (repr. Banner of Truth, 1974).

(4) Your paragraph at the bottom of page 2 beginning with the words 'The real difficulty' is a vital one. I feel that you are contrasting the teaching of Acts and the teaching of the Epistles in a wrong way. Surely the Epistles assume the teaching of Acts and really they cannot be understood apart from that. This I think is the major defect in your position. Remember also what we are told in Hebrews 2:4 and indeed in 1 Peter 1:11 and 12. The whole of the First Epistle to the Corinthians is meaningless apart from the background of Acts. How many churches do you know today to which it is necessary to write that Epistle?

(5) Page 3 on your MS where you deal with Schep's chapter 4 and the distinction between different types of Christians, I feel here that you are discounting entirely the difference between faith and the assurance of faith.[1] It is possible for a believer to be lacking in assurance, so that at any rate you have unbelievers, believers, and believers with full assurance. Is not the whole argument of 1 John really concerned with this, and especially the specific statement of Chapter 5, verse 13? Note also the different types of Chapter 2 of that Epistle. I feel that if you are right then in the light of the New Testament picture of the Christian as seen, e.g. in 1 Peter 1:8 that there are really very few Christians at all. What also of the argument in Gal. 4:15 – about 'Where is the blessedness ye spake of', and also Chapter 5:7. What also of the arguments against 'grieving and quenching the Spirit'? There were clearly people who were guilty of this and who had therefore lost something which they once had, but still they are Christians. This is also surely the point running through the Letters to the Churches in Rev. 2 and 3.

(6) Your page 5 dealing with Schep – page 31 second para: I feel you go too far here.[2] One reads of a remarkable experience which Thomas Aquinas had. Surely Luther also had exceptional

[1] Runia wrote, 'I see only one distinction in the NT: unbelievers and believers.'

[2] Runia criticised Schep's assertion that 'martyrs, reformers and numerous great saints' received the baptism with the Spirit and asked: 'How do you know? They never wrote about this. In their theology they never wrote about it either.'

experiences. There are certainly many in connection with some of the early Scotch Reformers, and there are many in the Puritans. I have found this in John Owen, Thomas Goodwin, John Flavel, John Howe and others. The language they use tends to vary but as to the experience it seems to be always the same. There is also the famous experience of Blaise Pascal, and also experiences of Jonathan Edwards and the other men of the 18th century. I venture to suggest that you are too much governed, perhaps, by the particular tradition in which you were nurtured. This is of course true of all of us no doubt.

(7) Your page 8 and 72 of Schep: I would not object to a criticism like this as I fear it is but true.[1] It is comparable to the preaching of the prophets in the Old Testament and the warnings of the Epistle to the Hebrews, and indeed the prophetic note in great preaching ever since.

(8) The final paragraph of your page 8: Surely the Confessions were concerned primarily with defining doctrine as over against the false teaching of Rome.[2] It is for that reason that those of us who stress their importance are ever in danger of falling into a scholasticism lacking in life and power. As you will know, this has happened many times in history, and that is what seems to call for repeated Revivals.

To sum up what I feel I would say that Prof. Schep is failing to 'prove and to test the spirits' while your danger is to 'quench the Spirit'. I feel that those in your position not only do not face that text but really more or less exclude it altogether.

Please forgive me for having written in such a dogmatic manner. I have done so in the interests of brevity and I know that you will understand.

May I say once more that I hope you will be given grace to bear with one another and to avoid any precipitate action. I am

[1] Runia complained that Schep's words on the 'traditional, respectable and in many respects lukewarm and formalistic church-life' of too many churches were 'harsh'.

[2] Runia referred to the absence of all 'baptism with the Spirit' teaching in the Confessions.

seriously considering, in the light of all that is happening with you, the possibility of publishing some 22 or 23 sermons which I preached on this matter.

May God grant great grace unto us all at this time of terrible confusion.

With warm regards to Mrs Runia and yourself,

Yours very sincerely,

D. M. Lloyd-Jones

P.S. I omitted to say that I agree with Prof. Schep on the use of the term 'second blessing'. Certainly in this country it is understood as referring to Sanctification.[1]

Faith Healing and Maynard James

49 Creffield Road,
Ealing, London W.5
18 September, 1969

[To Dr Gerald Golden]

My Dear Gerald,

Many thanks for your most kind letter. Strangely enough an almost identical one arrived from the authorities of the Sudan Interior Mission except that they had no reference to Maynard James's booklet.

With regard to the latter my attitude is this. He belongs to 'The Church of the Nazarenes' and they are very good people with whom I am in agreement apart from one thing, namely, that they believe the Baptism with the Holy Spirit confers entire sanctification. In other words they are really the followers of the teaching of John Wesley on holiness. When Maynard James originally sent me this booklet I pointed out of course our disagreement at this point but was able to say that I thought his terms of 'tongues' was

---

[1] All Reformed preachers rejected sanctification teaching on the 'victorious Christian life' which was to be entered by receiving a 'second blessing'. But Schep argued that what he was teaching could not be dismissed as 'second blessing' teaching in another form, for it dealt with full assurance, not sanctification.

excellent and balanced.

On this question of faith-healing I certainly agree with him. I expressed my disagreement with the view put in the Christian Medical Fellowship publication at the time. I think it is quite without scriptural warrant to say that all these gifts ended with the apostles or the apostolic era. I believe there have been undoubted miracles since then.[1] At the same time most of the claimed miracles by the Pentecostalists and others certainly do not belong to that category and can be explained psychologically or in other ways. I am also of the opinion that most, if not all, of the people claiming to speak in tongues at the present time are certainly under a psychological rather than a spiritual influence. But again I would not dare to say that 'tongues' are impossible at the present time.

I trust this will be of some help.

With much love to you both,

Martyn

The Baptism of the Spirit

49 Creffield Road,
Ealing, London W.5
1 November, 1969

[To Dr Gerald Golden]
Dear Gerald,

Many thanks for your letter. It seems clear to me that David Watson was quoting something probably he heard me preach.[2]

All I can send you at the moment is a sermon of mine in the *Westminster Record* for August 1968. This is, of course, but a summary of my teaching. I once preached a series of some 24

---

[1] ML-J believed it to be a Christian duty to believe in the possibility of healing, subject to God's will, but he strongly opposed the teaching that there is healing for all Christians if they will only believe and 'claim it' (*Romans: An Exposition of Chapter 8:5–17*, pp. 275–6).

[2] David Watson (1933–84), rector of St Cuthbert's, York, was possibly quoting words of Ml-J's preached 25 May 1961 and printed in the *Westminster Record*, September 1964, which criticised 'the very commonly held teaching today' that 'the baptism of the Spirit is non-experimental, that it

sermons on this subject and went into the matter in great detail, but I have not published them.[1]

If you can get hold of a copy of 'How to Study the Bible' by Dr R. A. Torrey and read the whole of his teaching on the Holy Spirit, but particularly the one dealing with the Baptism of the Spirit, you will find more or less what I believe, apart from the point of how this is to be 'received'.[2]

I do hope you will both have a good time in Thailand.

With much love to you both,

Yours very sincerely,

        D. M. Lloyd-Jones

---

happens to everybody at regeneration'. See Watson, *You Are My God* (London: Hodder and Stoughton, 1983), p. 57, and ML-J, *The Christian Warfare* (Edinburgh: Banner of Truth, 1976), p. 280, where the same sermon is published with slight revision. It is significant to note that his words were spoken before England heard anything of what was to be called 'the charismatic movement'.

[1] These twenty-four sermons were published posthumously as *Joy Unspeakable* (Eastbourne: Kingsway, 1984), and *Prove All Things* (Eastbourne: Kingsway, 1985), ed. C. Catherwood.

[2] It is extraordinary that at this date there was virtually nothing in print expounding the view of the Spirit's baptising work as experimental although it had once been the prevailing evangelical belief. It is significant that the historic view of the meaning of revival had also disappeared, hence the strength of ML-J's conviction that 'there is nothing that so quenches the Spirit as the teaching which identifies the baptism of the Holy Ghost with regeneration' (*The Christian Warfare*, p. 280) R. A. Torrey (1856–1928), American Congregational minister and evangelist, whose books were still read in evangelical circles, took the experimental view. But whereas ML-J held that larger givings of the Holy Spirit were sovereign acts of God, Torrey (and Pentecostalists who followed him) held that the 'baptism' could be received by the fulfilment of conditions. On ML-J and the charismatic movement see *D. Martyn Lloyd-Jones: The Fight of Faith*, pp. 474–91. It is regrettable that no full treatment of ML-J's position was in print until his *Romans: An Exposition of Chapter 8: 5–17* in 1974. For what he regarded as true and wrong understandings of the baptism of the Spirit see *The Puritans: Their Origins and Successors*, pp. 292–94, 312–13.

Fanaticism in Chard, Somerset

Rothiemurchus Manse,
Aviemore, Inverness-shire,
20 August, 1970

[To Dr Douglas Johnson]
My Dear Sir.

As Bethan and I stopped to have a snack at Pitlochry last Friday (14th) we were aware of an influence familiar, and yet strange in the setting. The arrival of your letter yesterday provided the explanation! [1]

We are here until the 31st D.V. and I am preaching on the Sundays. David Short and family were in the congregation last Sunday.

As to the business at Chard, several ministers have been in touch with me about it.[2] It is apparently a part of the Michael Harper movement but a particularly aggressive one. I fear that nothing can be done apart from helping people who are vaguely attracted and showing them the gross dangers and the thoroughly unscriptural character of the whole thing.

Hope you had a good holiday.

Warmest regards from us all to you all,

Yours,

D. M. Lloyd-Jones

[1] D. J. and his wife had been in the same place the preceding weekend.

[2] The charismatic movement was reaching the height of its influence at this date and the possession of spectacular 'gifts' had been claimed by a group at Chard, Somerset. D. J. had written to ML-J of numbers of students from London University going down to Chard on Friday evenings, sleeping in barns and neighbours' houses, and returning Sunday evening unfit for academic work the following day. In a personal note on this, D. J. informed us: 'Some of the girls began to get near breaking point. Those students attending Westminster and good churches could not do much because they were regarded as "unsound".' ML-J's response in this letter shows the absurdity of the view – deliberately spread by charismatics – that they had his sympathy.

Speaking in Tongues

49 Creffield Road,
Ealing, London W.5
17 May, 1971

[To Mr John Knight][1]
Dear Mr Knight,

Many thanks for your kind letter. I am very happy to answer your question; and it is simply this, that I have never spoken in Tongues either in private or in public.

It may be that I have met Dr Robert Banks but I cannot recall him.

With all good wishes,
Yours sincerely,
D. M. Lloyd-Jones

Preserving the Lives of Severely Handicapped Babies

49 Creffield Road,
Ealing, London W.5
7 November, 1973

[To Dr E. G. Gerald Roberts][2]
Dear Dr Roberts,

Many thanks for your most kind letter. I was so glad to have the pleasure of meeting you though it was but too brief. I hope that we shall be able to meet again at greater length.

I can well understand how you feel with these tremendous problems that confront you in your work at the present time, and it would really take a very long letter indeed to deal with this

[1] John Knight of Connels Point, Sydney, New South Wales. Mr Knight, hearing it claimed by an evangelical speaker in Australia that Lloyd-Jones 'had spoken in tongues, though he would never admit it in public', wrote to him to ascertain the truth.

[2] Consultant paediatrician at Wrexham who had written to ML-J concerning dilemmas which arose over preserving the lives of *spina bifida* babies.

situation in any adequate manner. The ideal method is Question and Answer.

The best I can do at the moment therefore is to lay down what I regard as the principles covering this whole matter.

(1) We must avoid the idea that the Bible is some kind of Ready Reckoner which we can turn up for an answer on these questions. As far as I am aware there is no single verse which deals with these problems and we therefore have to take the general tenor of the Biblical teaching.

(2) The Bible of course, tends not to envisage these problems in particular.

(3) The Law as given through Moses was meant to control life and conduct in general as between person and person, and not to answer more theoretical questions.

(4) The Law must not be interpreted in a mechanical or legalistic manner. I mean this. Some people say that there is really no difficulty at all about these questions which you have to face, because the Bible teaches 'Thou shalt not kill'. They feel that that settles it, but I argue that it doesn't, because that statement refers to the relationship between two persons one of whom may have a grudge against the other. It obviously does not cover the question of taking part in a war, for the God who issued that commandment also commanded the Children of Israel to kill and even to exterminate others.

(5) The Roman Catholics, I have always felt, have added greatly to our problems by adding their particular philosophical outlook to the teaching of the Scripture. They have made detailed statements which I feel have no scriptural warrant. Take for example the question of the origin of the soul, or the question as to when personality really begins.

(6) We are really left with the general teaching which is the great Commandment about Loving God, and our neighbour as ourselves and therefore desiring always the best for our neighbour as a person.

(7) We must always take the Biblical view of life in this world in the light of eternity. Many go astray because they regard this as the only life and world.

(8) There is no purpose in just perpetuating existence which is not real living.

(9) We should therefore always be satisfied that there are prospects of a more or less full life for the individual concerned as distinct from some kind of mechanical continuation of existence.

(10) We must always, if there is the slightest doubt or hesitation, give the benefit of the doubt to the patients.

In other words it ultimately becomes a matter of our judgment and wisdom, and as long as this is done honestly we can do no more. Thank God the eternal destiny of any soul is not in our hands and cannot be affected by what we decide.

I hope this will be of some little help to you. I need not say that I shall be glad to try to answer any questions you may care to put to me.

With my kindest regards,
Yours very sincerely,
D. M. Lloyd-Jones

Faith Healing and the CMF Memorandum

49 Creffield Road,
Ealing, London W.5
2 February, 1978

[To Dr Douglas Johnson]
My Dear Sir,

Your two letters arrived together this morning, so I hasten to reply.

1. I think the letter to the Editor of the *Journal of Medical Ethics* is good and deals very adequately with the main issue.

2. I shall be glad to read the Memorandum on Faith Healing as soon as you can let me have it.[1] I have just read two books by the

---

[1] This was a third revision of the work first put out as *A Memorandum on Faith Healing* (London: Christian Medical Fellowship, 1956), produced by the study group of the CMF which ML-J had chaired for some fifteen years. He did not agree with all its findings, as noted in his letter to

R.C. Father MacNutt and I must say that in many ways they have impressed me by their sanity and scripturalness.

Hope you are all well,

Warmest regards,

D. M. Lloyd-Jones

Observing Faith-Healing Conferences

49 Creffield Road,
Ealing, London W.5
23 March, 1978

[To Dr Douglas Johnson]

My Dear Sir,

Herewith the notices of Healing Conferences that are to be held.[1]

Here are my suggestions:

(1) Could not Scorer[2] or some such retired person attend as an observer and so find out exactly what is being taught and suggested? This would not commit him in any way.

Golden, above, of 18 September 1969. The revision now under discussion, upon which ML-J made a few corrections and asked for certain things to be verified, was published under the names of Vincent Edmunds and Gordon Scorer as *Some Thoughts on Faith Healing* (London: CMF, 1979). On miraculous healing see *D. Martyn Lloyd-Jones: The Fight of Faith*, pp. 785–88.

[1] ML-J had received notice and probably pressing invitations to these conferences shortly to be held, the main one organised by a leading group of charismatics. As had often happened through the years, he wanted D.J. to undertake reconnaissance and report results of enquiries. With increasing evidence of loose statements and of phoney cases of alleged healing coming to light, ML-J was especially concerned for accurate verification. Commenting on the attention the subject was receiving at this date, D.J. writes, 'Lots of people were all meeting to solve all mysteries of faith healing'.

[2] Gordon Scorer, a leader in the CMF study group.

(2) Is not [this] the opportunity to approach the leaders in this Movement, and those most interested, and ask them in the interests of truth and the welfare of many Christian patients, to urge all their members to keep careful records of all cases and make such available to the CMF when called for. It is really their duty to do this and they should be urged to do so. Those meeting at these conferences will probably be in touch with all other interested medical men everywhere.

Until Saturday, March 31st I shall be: c/o Catherwood, Sutton Hall, Balsham, Cambridge.

Warmest regards as ever,

D. M. Lloyd-Jones

9

THE 'RETIREMENT' YEARS

The Farewell Letter, 1968

Westminster Chapel,
Buckingham Gate,
London S.W.1.
Thursday, 30 May, 1968

[To the Members of Westminster Chapel]
My Dear Friends,

I am sending you, individually, this letter which is really addressed to the entire church. My feelings as I do so are naturally mixed; and I assure you that nothing but the clearest possible conviction that I am obeying the unmistakable will of God would lead me to write in this way.

On one matter, however, my feelings are not mixed, and that is in profound gratitude to you all for your prayers on behalf of my wife and myself during these past three months. I was deeply conscious of being upheld and was able to enjoy 'the peace of God that passeth all understanding'.

The object of this letter is to inform you that last night in a Deacons' meeting, I gave the Deacons 3 months' notice of my retirement from the pastorate of Westminster Chapel. In other words I shall not be resuming my ministry amongst you as intended next September.

I thank God that this decision is not based on considerations of health. My medical advisers assure me that I can regard myself as having had 'a complete surgical cure', and I am thankful to say that I am conscious of returning and increasing strength daily, and am already looking forward to fulfilling my various preaching engagements in various parts of the country, as from the first week in September. In other words, I am simply retiring from the pastoral charge of Westminster Chapel and hope to continue with all my other interests and activities.

My illness has simply acted as a precipitating factor in what was becoming an increasing conviction that I should take this step. However, owing to the wonderful and affectionate bonds that have bound us together for so long, I simply could not bring myself to do it. The moment I realised that I had to undergo an operation, I felt that God was saying to me, 'This is the end of one ministry and the beginning of another.' I said that to my dear wife and colleague before the operation, and, ever since, this conviction has deepened and become more and more clear.

The considerations that had weighed with me were the following. I am already past the age at which most people retire today. I have completed 30 unbroken years in the ministry of Westminster and given the best years of my life to it. This has meant that I have refused invitations from various parts of the world to lecture at colleges and seminaries and to address conferences of ministers, etc., etc. But, and perhaps most important of all, it has meant that I have only been able to publish but little of what I have preached at Westminster.[1] Great pressure has been brought to bear on me to publish more, and recently, increasing pressure to write some account of my spiritual pilgrimage and what it was that lead me over 41 years ago – to leave the medical profession and become a whole time preacher of 'the glorious gospel of the blessed God'.

It is because I am as certain that God has now called me to fulfil these tasks, as I was of His call 41 years ago, that I am taking this step and informing you of it.

As I said at the beginning, my feelings are mixed, inevitably so, and I cannot imagine what my life will be like without preaching

---

[1] He wrote to Philip Hughes on 6 July 1968: 'What really drove me to retire from Westminster was not so much my illness as the fact that I had been there for 30 years and that I have felt increasingly that I must put into book form more of the material that I have accumulated – for example, I am anxious to print what I have tried to do on the Epistle to the Romans among others.'

three times each week at Westminster Chapel – apart from my summer vacation. But when God calls, He is to be obeyed in spite of all natural feelings.

I know that you dear people will understand. If you do not, then my ministry has been in vain. I must not begin to write about the past and of the blessed and happy times that by the grace of God we have been allowed to have together. I cannot imagine a happier ministerial lot than mine has been. No minister could wish to have a more faithful and loyal people. I shall ever thank God for you all and those who have 'gone before'.

What things we have experienced! To a preacher nothing is so wonderful as to feel the unction of the Holy Spirit while preaching, and to hear of souls being brought under conviction of sin, and then experiencing the new birth. Thank God, that has often been our experience. But not only that, one remembers marriages, births, deaths, even war and bombing, reconstruction of buildings and many other matters faced together; but above all I shall treasure the privilege of ministering to those with grievous problems of various types and enjoying the trust and confidence of those passing through dark and deep waters.

But I must refrain. I know that you will all stand together and commit the future of our beloved church to God. It is His, not ours; and as He has led, He will continue to lead. As I have often reminded you, what happens at Westminster Chapel is observed and scrutinised far and wide, imitated and criticised. Your responsibility therefore is a very great one but I am confident that, as always in the past, you will face it, shoulder it, and rise to it in a manner that will bring great glory and honour to our blessed Lord and Saviour.

I need not assure you of my constant prayers and thoughts, and what applies to you will also apply to your new minister and leader.

Thus, with loving and most tender greetings from my wife and myself – what I and my ministry owe to her you all know – I subscribe myself for the last time.

Your privileged and unworthy minister and friend,
    D. M. Lloyd-Jones

Maintaining a Biblical Ministry at Westminster

49 Creffield Road,
Ealing, London W.5
March 29, 1969

[To the Rev. Eric J. Alexander]

My Dear Mr Alexander,

Please forgive me for writing this in my own illegible hand. But I cannot type, and the nature of this communication is such that I cannot dictate it to my usual helper.

I cannot tell you how grateful I am for your kindness and courtesy in sending me a copy of your letter to Omri Jenkins and also the personal word to me.[1]

I feel the position is now clarified, as it is clear from your letter to Omri Jenkins that you clearly perceive that the real problem is not the Westminster Fellowship but rather the attitude of the church at Westminster to these various problems.

---

[1] The Rev. Eric J. Alexander, of Newmilns Church of Scotland, Ayrshire, had been strongly urged by the Pastorate Committee dealing with the vacancy at Westminster Chapel to receive a call. In Mr Alexander's reply to the committee (chaired by the Rev. Omri Jenkins), he indicated his concern lest his acceptance of a call might lead to controversy at the Chapel. For he was not personally persuaded of the need to urge secession from the major, mixed, denominations and, while playing no part in the ecumenical movement himself, he would 'not be prepared to make a man's attitude to it a cardinal issue on which I would divide from him'. Out of deference to ML-J, and concern for the future unity of the Chapel, Mr Alexander had written to ML-J on 22 March and enclosed a copy of his reply to Mr Jenkins. A regrettable element of confusion seems to have attended this discussion for Dr Lloyd-Jones himself was to maintain fellowship with ministers in the Church of England and the Church of Scotland provided they did not support ecumenism. The BEC had become identified with a policy of secession and Westminster Chapel was a key factor in the growth of its influence. Mr Alexander became minister of St. George's-Tron, Glasgow, in 1977.

As regards the Fellowship, as I told you several times there was no real problem, as I would have been quite happy for you not to belong to it, though naturally regretting that.

At this point I therefore cease to be implicated. From the beginning I have not taken any part in the direct affairs of the chapel, and I only came in at your request over the matter of the Fellowship which Omri Jenkins rightly said had nothing to do with the chapel.

Now, on the purely personal level, I want you to know that I fully understand how you feel, and respect your position.

Once more, however, I would venture to urge you to give the fullest possible consideration to the need of maintaining a biblical ministry at Westminster. For myself I would be prepared to sacrifice almost everything for that.

I cannot believe that you will allow perfectly natural traditional ties or considerations of friendships and associations to govern your decision as over against that overwhelming consideration. Again I would press upon you the element of duty in this matter. Whether the Church of Scotland or any other church can be won for evangelicalism is at best a matter of speculation and possibility; but what a man like you could do at Westminster, under God, is a certainty.

I shall continue to pray most urgently for you and the church, that God may over-rule all to His glory and praise.

With my warmest regards and greetings,

Yours very sincerely,

D. M. Lloyd-Jones

Her Husband's Death, a 'Grievous Blow to Wales'

at 59A Walnut St,
Jenkintown,
Pa., 19046
April 26, 1969

[To Mrs John B. E. Thomas][1]
Dear Eluned,

I shall never forget what I felt last night when Elizabeth told me the shattering news of the passing of your dear one. Bethan and I still cannot realize that it is true. It seems quite impossible for he appeared to be unusually well when I was with you a month ago.

There is so much that I would like to say and could say. Perhaps the greatest thing of all is that in my opinion he was of all the younger men in Wales the one whom we could not afford to lose. Ever since I first met him as a student I formed the highest opinion of him, his character, his ability and his leadership. He more than fulfilled this throughout the years and one looked forward to yet greater things in the years to come. It is a most grievous blow to the whole evangelical cause in Wales and to all of us who knew him and loved him. But God's ways are not our ways and He knows best, though we cannot understand.

All of us who knew you both well can realize what this means to you. You had continued to be lovers though married for years and you were so perfectly suited to each other.

Thank God you know to whom to turn and He will not fail you. All we can do is to continue praying for you. It grieves me much that I cannot be at the funeral to pay my tribute to him, but I am glad to think that he knew what I thought of him.

With loving and deepest sympathy,
Yours very sincerely,
D. M. Lloyd-Jones

---

[1] The Rev. John B. E. Thomas (1927–69), minister of Sandfields, Aberavon, since 1953, and one of the leaders of the Evangelical Movement of Wales had died suddenly on 25 April at the age of forty-

The Death of John Thomas

Westminster Theological Seminary,
Chestnut Hill,
Philadelphia 18,
Pennsylvania,
U S A
14 May, 1969

[To the Rev. Geoffrey Thomas][1]
My dear Friend,

Many thanks for your kind and unexpected letter.

My wife and I were particularly glad to get it because of your wonderful account of the funeral service for our dear friend, John Thomas. It grieved me much that I could not be there as I have known him since he was a student and was really responsible for introducing him to the church. As you say, this is a grievous loss and means that those of us who remain will have to stand together in the fight more than ever.

I am having a most happy time here and have just delivered my fourteenth lecture, each lasting one hour. I am hoping that there will be time for discussion at the last two lecture periods next week when I finish on the 21st.

I hope you are both well. With my warmest regards.

Yours very sincerely,

D. Martyn Lloyd-Jones

---

one. See *Contender for the faith, a tribute to the Rev J. B. E. Thomas*, including an introductory memoir by Graham Harrison (Briton Ferry: Evangelical Movement of Wales, 1975).

[1] Minister of Alfred Place Baptist Church, Aberystwyth, from 1965.

Generosity Shared

Apt 210-B
The Regency,
2444 Madison Road,
Cincinnati,
Ohio
[June 1969]

[To Mr and Mrs H. F. R. Catherwood]
My dear Fred and Elizabeth,

I have not gone mad suddenly. This is but passing on to you some of the generosity shown to us.

You will be glad to know that I have started work on correcting my sermons on The Epistle to the Romans. I have already done 9! The work on Ephesians 2 is nearing completion. I am hoping to talk to various publishers at the Religious Books Exhibition which is to be held here the last week in this month.[1]

You have been having all other news so I will say no more. Fondest love to you all,

Ever yours,

Father

P.S. I am sending the same amount to Keith and Ann. I got it changed into £ in order to save any fuss and bother your end. [Bethan Lloyd-Jones added: 'We would like the children to have a fiver – £5 – each out of this *now!* for their holiday or whatever.']

---

[1] This summer he made major decisions on his future publishers. His first volume on Ephesians (*God's Way of Reconciliation)* went to the Evangelical Press and Moody (1972), his first on Romans (*An Exposition of Chapters 3.20–4.25)* to Zondervan and Banner of Truth (1970). Subsequently the Banner of Truth were given both series in the UK.

News of Books

49 Creffield Road,
Ealing, London W.5
16 February, 1972

[To Dr Philip E. Hughes]
My Dear Philip,

Your most beautiful and useful calendar diary arrived safely this morning and we were naturally delighted to receive it. Why it should have taken all this time in transit I do not know, but things seem to go from bad to worse. It will be good to have this constant reminder of you.

I need not say that you are very frequently in our thoughts. I do hope that you will keep me informed of any developments that may take place.

I am glad to say that we are all well. The Lectures which I delivered at the Seminary have already been published in this country under the title of *Preaching and Preachers* by Hodder and Stoughton. It will soon appear in the USA published by Zondervan. I shall ask them to send you a copy the moment it appears. I think it will interest you.

I am very busy at the present time preparing the MS for my third volume on the Epistle to the Romans. This deals with chapter 6 and is, of course, the volume in which I deal directly with the Keswick teaching without mentioning the term.

I hope that you are near the end of your Commentary on Hebrews to which I look forward most eagerly.

I am glad to say that we are all well in spite of strikes, power cuts and various other troubles.

We all join in sending our love and warmest greetings to you three.

Yours very sincerely,
D. M. Lloyd-Jones

Discussion of Publications

49 Creffield Road,
Ealing, London W.5
3 October, 1975

[To the Rev. Iain H. Murray]
My Dear Friend,

I return herewith O. R. J's article[1] and the children's book. Here are my comments:

1. I would *not* publish Johnston's article for many reasons. Actually I disagree with most of the argument. He is wrong historically when he says that Christians were right in the early part of the 19th century and then went wrong. Actually it was in the second half, when they began preaching the social gospel, and forming temperance and moral societies etc, that the rot came in. Surely the Church of Scotland and the Free Church [of Scotland] through the years have done the very thing he is advocating. I well remember Finlayson's articles in the *Record* when he was editor.[2] They were often quoted in London papers derisively and as jokes! Above all, he completely fails to see that the Wilberforces and the Shaftesburys can only succeed after times of Revival when there are

---

[1] O. R. Johnston (1927–85), Director of Care Campaigns, had spoken at the 1975 Leicester Ministers' Conference on Christian action on moral and social issues in contemporary society. The substance of his address, offered to us for publication, I had sent on to ML-J for his opinion. It was subsequently published by Paternoster Press (Exeter: 1976) under the title, *Christianity in a Collapsing Culture*. ML-J was all too aware of the declining moral conditions but, as this letter shows, he regarded the new Anglican evangelical emphasis on this theme as misconceived for it was passing over the fundamental cause of the nation's problems. He also saw that willingness to make common cause with non-evangelicals on moral questions was liable to undermine the distinctive evangelical position on what is of greatest importance. Johnston, it should be said, worked hard for reformation at all levels in the Church of England.

[2] Professor R. A. Finlayson (1895–1989), Editor of the Free Church of Scotland's *Monthly Record* 1937–58).

many Christians. The Religious Societies of 1664–1735 achieved practically nothing etc., etc. Page 15 (mid) about Brethren is sheer confusion and just a defence of his own position. I also object to quoting Vidler and several others. The real trouble with these Anglican evangelicals is that they only began to get out of their ghettos about 1960 and are still utterly ignorant of non-conformity from 1860 onwards.[1]

2. Children's book. I entirely agree with you.[2] This might very well have been published by CSSM or even worse. I have always disliked this kind of thing and for the Free Church to publish it is ridiculous.

Love to you all,

Yours,

    D. M. Lloyd-Jones

On the Death of her Husband

49 Creffield Road,
Ealing, London W.5
21 November, 1977

[To Mrs J. Gwyn-Thomas][3]

My Dear Nancy,

Though I know that words are totally inadequate I feel I must write on behalf of all of us as a family to let you know how deeply we feel for you and Christopher and Elizabeth in your irreparable loss. The news came as a great shock to us and we feel it is almost incredible.

---

[1] From that period moral and social action had gradually become the main part of Nonconformist witness in England, during which time its real spiritual influence was in rapid decline.

[2] I had sent him some material produced for children by the Free Church of Scotland's Publications Committee and to which some of us had unsuccessfully objected.

[3] John Gwyn-Thomas, Vicar of St Paul's, Cambridge, had died unxpectedly at the age of fifty-four.

I feel I have lost a very dear and valued friend. I can say quite truthfully that there was no man whom I looked forward to meeting more than him, or anyone whose company I so greatly enjoyed always.

God's ways are beyond our understanding but we know that they are always good and right. He alone can help and strengthen you; and He has promised to do so. All we your friends can do is to pray for you, and we shall do so.

With most loving sympathy from Bethan, Ann and myself,

Yours very sincerely,

Martyn Lloyd-Jones

The Ephesians Series

at Balsham,
24 August, 1978

[To the Rev. Iain H. Murray]

My Dear Friend,

Herewith the Preface for *God's Ultimate Purpose*.[1] I felt that I must give an explanation of the order in which these books have appeared and also give advance notice of those that are to follow. You, no doubt, will probably draw attention somewhere to the fact that, ultimately, D.V., the entire Epistle will be covered.

We were delighted to have you here last week and glad to know that you got home safely.

Incidentally you were right about the date of the sermons in

---

[1] *God's Ultimate Purpose: An Exposition of Ephesians 1:1 to 23* (Edinburgh: Banner of Truth, 1978). Although this volume deals with chapter one of the epistle, it was the fifth to appear in his series on Ephesians. He had not originally anticipated a demand for all his sermons on the epistle. The seventh and concluding volume (on chapter 4:17 to 5:17) was published in 1982, the year after his death and the whole series remains available today.

Chapter 3 – it was January–April 1957! I was thinking of the date of the first sermon which was 1956.[1]

Our love to you as a family,

Yours very sincerely,

D. M. Lloyd-Jones

P.S. Bethan has made the fair copy of the Preface for obvious reasons![2]

Dallimore on Whitefield, volume 2

as from, 49 Creffield Road,
Ealing, London W.5
8 January, 1979

[To the Rev. Iain Murray]

My Dear Friend,

Herewith the pages from Dallimore's MS on which I have made pencilled alternative suggestions. Also my notes in margins of your letter to Mr Houghton.[3] Hope you will be able to decipher both!

I am quite certain that you should publish this volume. It should do great good not only in re-establishing the leadership of G.W. in the Evangelical Awakening but also in correcting the false picture which the Wesleyans have propagated for two centuries. I am actually much impressed at D's effort to be fair and judicial!

Loving greetings to you all,

Yours very sincerely,

D. M. Lloyd-Jones

---

[1] I had pointed out a slip we had overlooked in the Preface to his sermons on Ephesians 3:1 to 21 where he dated all those sermons as preached in 1956. Those from verse 17 came in 1957.

[2] He did not type and his handwriting caused bewilderment to many.

[3] Mr S. M. Houghton and myself had been concerned over some points in the text of the MS by Dr Arnold Dallimore of his second volume on *George Whitefield*. The first volume had been published by us in 1970, with a Preface by ML-J. The second volume appeared in 1980. ML-J was deeply interested in all such matters.

The Bala Conference

49 Creffield Road,
Ealing, London W.5
17 July, 1979

[To the Rev. Elwyn Davies]
Dear Friend,

Many thanks for your kind letter. I am very glad to hear that the Conference in Bala has been so successful. As far as I can see the dates you suggest for 1980 are right for me, i.e. the week that begins on Sunday June 29th.[1]

So far I cannot remember anything historical which ought to be given attention in 1980. If I remember anything I will let you know.

I hope you are all well and that you will have happy and blessed Conferences at Aberystwyth in August.

Warmest regards as always,
Ever truly,
D. M. Lloyd-Jones

Fulfilling a Preaching Engagement

49 Creffield Road,
Ealing, London W.5
6 September, 1979

[To Pastor Douglas D. Jones]
Dear Friend,

Many thanks for your kind letter.[2]

Let me tell you the position. I have not been too good this summer and really began to wonder whether I could be with you after all. I have already cancelled Corsham feeling it would be too

---

[1] His health was to prevent a fulfillment of this engagement.

[2] Douglas Jones of Trinity Baptist Church, Gloucester, and a long-time member of the Westminster Fellowship, had invited ML-J to preach at the 25th anniversary of his pastorate at Trinity and was now writing to clarify

much for me and all Shepshed [services] next Sunday (9th) and the ministers meeting at Hinckley on the 10th. However, I hope to be with you and especially in view of your kindness in offering to come for me on Saturday the 15th.

My wife I fear will not be with me, but she, and I, deeply appreciate your good lady's kindness in inviting her.

What about coming to tea on the 15th, and then we can set off together.

I hope you are both well.

My wife joins me in sending our warmest regards and greetings,

Yours sincerely,

D. M. Lloyd-Jones

The Right Attitude to Controversy

49 Creffield Road,
Ealing, London W.5
19 March, 1980

[To Mr Ron L. Riseborough][1]

Dear Friend,

Many thanks for sending the article in *New Life* by Carl McIntire's camp-follower. It is typical of their mentality and unworthy of a reply.

---

arrangements. ML-J's willingness not to disappoint him typically overcame the very real concern there was for his health by this date. He was to preach at least eight times in October and for a last time at Westminster Chapel on 7 November. From December 1979 he accepted no public engagements but then, to the wonder and joy of his friends, he spoke and preached in a number of places between April 28 and 7 June 1980.

[1] The recipient of this letter, once a member of Westminster Chapel, had emigrated to Melbourne, Australia, at the end of the 1960s. The article from *New Life* (Melbourne) which he had sent to ML-J probably criticised Dr Lloyd-Jones for lack of any involvement in the anti-ecumenical stance of the International Council of Christian Churches (ICCC), founded by Dr Carl McIntire.

I refused to co-operate with them because of their spirit and their methods back in 1946.[1]

The thing to ask this friend is as to whether McIntire has any supporters by now in the USA apart from his own church. Poole Connor and Bishop Thompson[2] left them fairly soon after I did feeling very disillusioned. Francis Schaeffer who was sent to me by McIntire in 1946 has also left him years ago.[3] But perhaps one of the most striking cases is that of Allan MacRae a 1st class OT scholar and principal of a theological college who held on until but a few years back and then left, until by now McIntire is isolated and almost alone. All have left him for the same reason.

On the positive side we now have here in England the British Evangelical Council which is quite a strong body and maintaining a powerful anti-ecumenical witness, and we have also started the London Theological Seminary to do the same and to withstand the trend to Rome. What has the ICCC to shew of comparable worth.

I knew T. T. Shields of Toronto and refused to co-operate with him for the same reason. At the end of his life he also had lost most of his supporters. These men are tragedies and to be pitied. I would certainly not enter into controversy with them. Incidentally Ockenga has not preached in Westminster Chapel since 1956 or 7. I never sponsored the Graham campaigns and was the only

[1] This may be a slip of memory. The ICCC was founded in 1948.

[2] E. J. Poole-Connor, founder of the Fellowship of Independent Evanglical Churches (FIEC), and D. A. Thompson who had been a bishop in the Free Church of England. With five others they founded the BEC as a British witness against ecumenism in 1953.

[3] Again the date was probably 1948. A good statement of the position which Schaeffer (1912–84) came to hold can be found in his book *The Church Before the Watching World* (London: IVP, 1972), where he writes: 'If we stress the love of God without the holiness of God, it turns out only to be compromise. But if we stress the holiness of God without the love of God, we practise something which is hard and lacks beauty . . . I came to the conclusion that in the flesh we can stress purity without love or we can stress the love of God without the purity, but that in the flesh we cannot stress both simultaneously' (p. 54).

evangelical in London not to do so. But I did not simply denounce him negatively and with bitterness. It is our duty to help and persuade men and shew them a better way.

I have been unwell since early December but am now beginning to improve. Please forgive the writing, but Mrs Burney[1] is in hospital.

Hope you are all well as a family.

With warmest regards and greetings from us all,

Yours very sincerely,

    D. M. Lloyd-Jones

Helping the Next Generation

49 Creffield Road,
Ealing, London W.5
9 August, 1980

[To Mr Wallace Crichton][2]

Dear Mr Crichton,

I do not know how to thank you for your extremely kind letter and for the fact that you troubled to write it. It has come to me not only with great joy but also with very great encouragement.

My health has not been good during the whole of this year and I have not preached at all since the beginning of June; so your letter came at a most appropriate time.

There is no greater privilege in life than to be of some help to such men as your two sons. I rejoice to hear of the way in which God has so greatly blessed them and I am sure that they are going

---

[1] His part-time secretarial helper.

[2] Mr Wallace Crichton, of Broughty Ferry, Dundee, who had formerly lived in London. He wrote to ML-J after going to the ordination of his younger son in the United States. On that occasion this son had said before a number of others, 'Dad, do you know the best thing you ever did for John and I?' On Mr Crichton responding that he did not, he was told, 'Taking John and me to hear Dr Martyn Lloyd-Jones'. Informing me of this, the father added: 'They had been brought up with the open Brethren. But they literally sat at the Doctor's feet.'

to be greatly used to His Glory.

When you next write to them will you please convey to them my warmest loving greetings and tell them that their story has warmed my heart. I pray that God will bless them more and more and give them increasing joy in His service. I pray the same for you.

With warmest greetings,

Yours very sincerely,

      D. M. Lloyd-Jones

News of ML-J's Health

49 Creffield Road,

Ealing, London W.5

29 October, 1980

[To Dr Gerald Golden]

My Dear Gerald,

How kind of you to write to Bethan and show such loving concern for me – indeed for us both.

I believe I have told you that I had to have my prostate removed four years ago. All went well until last May when I had a recurrence and was operated upon on June 10. Since then I have been going into hospital every three weeks for chemotherapy and stay in from one night to a week. I am actually due in again this next Friday.

We cannot tell you how much we appreciate your true brotherliness and concern. Your letter brought back happy and treasured memories – we have never ceased to thank God for you and Dorothy and for all the difference you made to us during the early days of the war.

We shall greatly value your prayers.

God bless you in all your ways, my dear Gerald,

With our love,

Yours ever,

      Martyn

New Experiences and Faith

49 Creffield Road,
Ealing, London W.5
4 December, 1980

[To the Rev. Ron Clarke][1]
My Dear Friend,

I cannot tell you what your letter of ten days ago did to me and meant to me. The very fact that in your present state of health you should ever have thought of writing moved me deeply and your wonderful account of the service at Westminster Chapel years ago both humbled and raised me up full of praise to our gracious God. How good of you to have done this.

We have both been passing through new experiences and I am sure that you feel as I do that finally nothing matters but the fact that we are in God's hands. We and our works are nothing. It is His choosing us before the foundation of the world that matters and He will never leave us nor forsake us. More and more do I see that what we need is a simple child-like faith, just to believe His word and surrender ourselves to Him utterly.

I pray that He may bless you and your dear family more and more and that you will soon be restored to continue your ministry. I thank God for you.

With loving Christian greetings to you three,
Yours ever sincerely,
D. M. Lloyd-Jones

---

[1] Minister of Buckingham Chapel, Clifton, from 1966. Mr Clarke's account of the effect of a service at Westminster Chapel when he was a student for the ministry was published in the *Banner of Truth*, March 1981, pp. 8–10.

Last Testimony and Greetings

49 Creffield Road,
Ealing, London W.5
22 January, 1981

[To Dr Philip E. Hughes][1]

My Dear Philip,

I send just a word to thank you for your most kind letter which arrived just before Christmas. I deeply value your loving interest in me and your prayers.

My health is still very much the same and I have not been able to preach or do anything else since the beginning of June. I thank God for all His bountiful goodness to me over the long years, and for all He has graciously allowed me and enabled me to do. My supreme desire now is to testify more than ever to the glory and wonder of His grace. I shall greatly value your prayers that I may be given strength to do so to His glory.

I am glad to say that God in a marvellous manner is granting Bethan most remarkable health and vigour. He is indeed a gracious God.

We both join in sending our loving regards and greetings to you both, and to Marian.

Yours ever sincerely,
D. M. Lloyd-Jones

---

[1] This letter concluded a correspondence which had continued regularly over forty years. Dr Philip Hughes died in Pennsylvania in 1990.

A Farewell Note

49 Creffield Road,
Ealing, London W.5
22 January, 1981

[To Professor R. Strang Miller][1]

Dear Professor Miller,

Please forgive me for this delay in writing to thank you for your most kind letter received just before Christmas. I need not say that I deeply value your encouraging words about my volumes on Romans and Ephesians.

I well remember our meeting in Mrs Andre's home and have been interested in you and all you have done ever since.

Unfortunately, my health has not been too good during the past year and I have not been able to preach or do anything else since the beginning of June. I will greatly value your prayers.

May God bless you and yours more and more in every respect.

Yours very sincerely,

D. M. Lloyd-Jones

---

[1] The Rev. R. S. Miller had been in England with the New Zealand forces in 1941–42 and had maintained a link with ML-J thereafter. He was at this date Professor of Church History at the Theological College of the Presbyterian Church of Australia in Melbourne. In a letter of 16 December 1980, Miller had described himself as 'one of the many who, under God,' owed him 'more than they can say, especially for your ministry through the printed page in the last decade or so.'

Thanks to an Author

49 Creffield Road,
Ealing, London W.5
11 February, 1981

[To the Rev. Alan C. Clifford][1]
Dear Friend,

Many thanks for your kindness in sending my wife and myself the cassette. We much appreciate your loving thoughts of us at the present time and are encouraged by them.

I believe you have provided a good general introduction to 'The Story of the Church' and I hope it will stimulate many to start reading. I need not say that I am very grateful for your kind and generous references to me. They have encouraged me. We both join in sending our loving Christian greetings to you both and the family.

Your sincerely,
D. M. Lloyd-Jones

---

[1] Member of the Westminster Fellowship and minister at Great Ellingham in Norfolk. This short letter, written less than a month from his death and when his sickness was far advanced, illustrates how he sought to strengthen the hands of younger men in the gospel ministry to the very last. ML-J had been in the homes of many such men and always maintained an interest in their families.

The Future of the Westminster Fellowship

49 Creffield Road,
Ealing, London W5
11 February, 1981

[To the Rev. John A. Caiger]¹

[To the Rev. John A. Caiger][1]
My dear Friend,

Many thanks for your letter of the 6th. It was just what I wanted and it is good of you to have done this.

Hywel Jones will have told you of our talk on the phone yesterday, but I believe it is right that it should be in writing as well. I am glad that the men adopted most of the suggestions.

I still believe that the large committee should be appointed because it will be very representative. Out of these I would have an Executive committee of six – two from the provincial gatherings consisting of Chairman, and either the Secretary, or someone else they may prefer; two from the Theological Seminary consisting of the Acting Chairman of the committee, and one other (as the Secretary here is a layman I would suggest the Rev. Graham Harrison); two from the Westminster Conference committee, you

---

[1] Mr Caiger (minister of Gunnersby Baptist Church, London) had joined the Fellowship c.1943–44 and had long acted as its secretary. In a letter to me of 29 September 1981 he gives this comment on a difference in the Fellowship as he remembered it: 'In the early years the Doctor invariably sat in his chair and never moved. He said relatively little, except by way of comment and criticism, and any summing up was very brief. The sessions had much more a judicial flavour as if we were members of a legal commission or witnesses presided over by one of His Majesty's High Court Judges. But, as you know, with the passing of the years the sessions became increasingly pastoral, with the Doctor on his feet more and more, virtually preaching to us and sharing with us a great wealth of his experience as a Christian and a preacher.'

as Chairman and Peter Lewis.[1] You should be permanent Chairman of the General and Executive committees – I suggest also that a new Secretary be appointed to do the donkey work which you have done for so many years and so graciously.

The Executive committee will select subjects and speakers for the various meetings. Of course, as regards subjects, suggestions will be made to them from time to time, but as regards speakers, I suggest that they always choose the man concerned. They should confine their choice in general to the members of the General committee, but if there is someone with a particular interest outside, they should be at liberty to choose him.

I suggest that this procedure be adhered to for at least five years. It will avoid all elections and nominations, and also avoid members being carried away by someone who will only be of temporary interest. It will also give time for natural leaders to appear.

At the end of five years if desired, the whole matter may be reconsidered and either continued, modified, or changed.

I would emphasise again that these are but suggestions made in response to the men's request to me.

Please convey my warmest love and greetings to all, and assure them of my daily prayers, both in their own churches and in the Fellowship. I believe the Fellowship is going to play a vital part in the coming years, and I am sure that God is going to bless it greatly and use it. I need not say that I have regarded it as one of the greatest privileges of my life to be actively concerned in it for so long, and I express my warm gratitude to all the men for their loyalty and loving patience with me.

Ever yours sincerely,
D. M. Lloyd-Jones

P.S. My wife joins me in sending our love as ever to you both.

---

[1] The three groups here mentioned, namely, men from provincial ministers' fraternals who also belonged to the Westminster Fellowship, from the faculty of the London Theological Seminary, and from the Westminster Conference committee, represented those with whom ML-J was most closely associated. He saw that much would depend upon their continued

[The above letters of 11 February were probably the last that he dictated. His mind remained entirely lucid, and he was never confined to bed, but by February 24 he was so weak that he could hardly speak. A few days later his speech was gone. In a shaky hand, he wrote on a scrap of paper for Bethan and the family, 'Do not pray for healing. Do not hold me back from the glory.' By smiles and gestures he was able to continue to express himself until in the early morning of Sunday, 1 March 1981 the day broke and all shadows fled away.

'This is my final comfort and consolation in this world. My only hope of arriving in glory lies in the fact that the whole of my salvation is God's work.'[1]

'It is grace at the beginning, grace at the end. So that when you and I come to lie upon our deathbeds, the one thing that should comfort and help and strengthen us there is the thing that helped us at the beginning. Not what we have been, not what we have done, but the grace of God in Jesus Christ our Lord. The Christian life starts with grace, it must continue with grace, it ends with grace. Grace, wondrous grace. "By the grace of God I am what I am." "Yet not I, but the grace of God which was with me."'[2]]

---

unity. Commenting in a letter to me (3 April 1983) on this last letter from ML-J, John Caiger wrote: 'It bears testimony to the Doctor's love for the Fellowship, his pastoral concern for ministers, and the humility of spirit which inspired him to view this ministry as such a great privilege.'

[1] ML-J, *Sanctified Through the Truth* (Kingsway: Eastbourne, 1989), p. 49.

[2] ML-J, *Spiritual Depression: its Causes and Cure* (Pickering and Inglis: London, 1965), p. 132.

INDEX

[239]

Dr. Martin Lloyd Jones at Merthyr

"ONE OF OUTSTANDING PREACHERS OF OUR TIME"

Large congregations gathered on Wednesday last to listen to the Rev. Dr. Martin Lloyd Jones preaching at Pontmorlais C.M. Church.

It is inspiring to see in these days of dwindling interest in religion that there are ministries that attract and hold the attention of great numbers of people. Undoubtedly people came from the surrounding districts to listen to this famous preacher, but this only gives force to the contention that the Christian Gospel can command a following.

Dr. Jones has been in Merthyr many times, but his following does not diminish. It is sometimes suggested that his romantic entry into the ministry accounts for his popularity. Most people have forgotten that he left Harley-street at the height of his career to become the minister of a mission church at

A marathon lecture

The one totally unequivocal London celebration of the Great Ejectment, of 1662, may well prove, when the tercentenary year ends, to have been neither that of the Unitarians in the spring nor the meetings planned by the Free Church majority for August and October but a remarkable gathering in the Welsh Church, Chiltern Street, on Tuesday night, for the annual lecture of the Evangelical Library. The lecturer was Dr Martyn Lloyd-Jones, of Westminster Chapel, and he gave a marathon performance of 2¼ hours.

The church, its porch, and a small room behind were packed with men and women of all age groups. After he had read for two hours, Dr Lloyd-Jones's voice seemed not to have flagged a
from a
the whol
"Milton,
this hou
thee," an
which Ch
the "fen
Wordswo
Dr Lloyd
of today.
there. A
but the g
"Our fa
men, who
receive t

Hundreds turned away from Swansea church

Dr. Martin Lloyd Jones, the famous divine, preached to packed congregations at Mount Pleasant Church yesterday.

The afternoon congregation was asked not to come to the evening service so that other people could have a chance, but the doors had to be closed at six p.m., and hundreds of people were turned away.

SWANSEA QUEUE TO HEAR FAMOUS PREACHER

Fish queues, tomato queues, and queues for the cinema are commonplace these days, but it is a rare sight to see a queue outside a chapel.

Such was the case in Swansea on Sunday when, for quite an hour before the doors of Argyle Chapel, St. Helen's-road, were opened, a long queue waited outside the building.

The occasion was the first anniversary of the minister, the Rev. D. Reginald Thomas, and the special preacher was Dr. Martin Lloyd Jones, of Westminster Chapel, London.

Seats were placed in the aisle and many people stood the service around the y, but even so hundreds turned away.

Martin Lloyd Jones, who eded Dr. Campbell Mort Westminster, is famed

An Appeal To Turn To The Gospel

DR. MARTIN LLOYD JONES'S INSPIRING ADDRESS

The unfavourable weather did not prevent a large number of people gathering in Windsor Road Congregational Church, Barry, to hear an inspiring address from Dr. Martin Lloyd Jones, of Westminster Chapel, London.

In this address he spoke on "The Gospel of Jesus Christ," and took as his text Jeremiah 6, 16: "Thus saith the Lord, ask for the old paths, where is the good way, and walk therein in . . ." These words were spoken at a time of national crisis, and of religious and spiritual decline, closely paralleled in this land today. From them he pointed out the inevitable law of history—Disobey God, and political crisis and moral decline are sure to follow. Without this fear of God, political alliances will avail nothing, either in the days of Jeremiah or in the present day.

The only solution to present day world problems lies in a return to God, and in the acceptance of what Jesus of Nazareth has offered man this last 2,000 years. Jesus is offered as the solution; His life

War Has Altered M Of People

Declares Greatest

"THE most s amongst us c hide from themselv that the war has ne greater seriousness i of the people," decl Martin Lloyd-Jones dress to more than people at Heath Welsh Chapel, Wa Monday.

The service was re schoolroom, so great we who besieged the Chape greatest preacher in Wales to-day.

Dr. Lloyd-Jones is promising evangelical, a Street specialist who brilliant medical career preach the gos pulpit of the Morgan at

on the text can discern th f the earth;

RELIGIO WIV

Over Dr.

PEOPLE T

A thousand llscombe Sec on Wednesda Martyn Llc one of the n Bible teache and coaches Weston-supe Minehead, T Exeter, conv and people ing, filling t and stage, an joining clas loudspeaker

Dr. G. E. Wivelliscomb conducted th prised hymn reading, and

Dr. Kelly privilege to with them.